Oofle Dust

The Story of Albert le Bas
Ireland's Foremost Magical
Entertainer

ORLA KELLY
PUBLISHING

Barbara le Bas

with Chris Woodward

Albert

and

Betty
Le Bas

Dedicated to their memory with love.

For the concert of life, no one has a programme…

Contents

FOREWORD

───────❧───────

Once Only...

Albert Le Bas was a magician. He was, in fact, one of the foremost professional magicians in the world. A man at the apex of one of the most ancient and honoured crafts in entertainment. But his accomplishments went far beyond mere tricks and legerdemain.

Albert or Bertie Le Bas' real magic lay in the way he could light up the eyes of children, in the way he could warm up the hearts of all he met, in the way he could leave us, not only laughing, but feeling for a little while that this old world was not such a bad place to live in after all.

For this magic, Bertie needed no top hat nor anything but his own warm and generous nature. Only once in a lifetime do you meet a man like Albert Le Bas. His magic tricks were real, because his real magic was in that kind and empathetic nature which we, who make the stage the centre of our world, will especially miss.

This Memorial Concert is our tribute to him, to a man who himself was always first to proffer his services to any worthy cause. It is the only sort of memorial that showbusiness believes in, a small offering of the collective talents of his fellow artists to an outstanding member of the profession. This memorial is not a solemn one. It is a tribute of music and song, laughter and gaiety – the only kind of memorial that would appeal to Bertie Le Bas who lived all of his gentle life in this way, in that kind of world and contributed so much to it.

Go laghduigh Dia an phian da lion tight le h-imtheacht aimsire. (May God lessen the pain of his loss to his family with the passage of time)

The above foreword was really the introduction in the theatre programme for the Albert Le Bas Memorial Concert that was held at the Gaiety Theatre, Dublin on October 22nd, 1972. Albert had passed away in the previous month. Obviously, no time had been lost in arranging this special and unique event. All the charitable warm-hearted souls and friends of Albert appeared on stage and those in the audience were there to remember him that night with the greatest affection. Betty and the children were also there.

Within the pages of the programme were some really beautiful words written by Irish poet and author Peter Mooney (AKA Pete St John) that I do feel are worth repeating here and are reproduced with his permission.

ALBERT LE BAS

Life looked past the patience of his eyes
and laid its fragile magic mantle down
making prisoners of the privileged ones
who saw his art and stopped to know the man.

The stage transformed to wonder and to awe
his unassuming presence marked the change
when disbelieving eyes and blunted hearts
a little while rejoiced in strange suspension.

Le Bas, Le Bas, as if it were a chant
and magic in profundity awoke
and human values fled before his touch
to make again small children of our hearts

And those who worked the boards
and share the bill
or joined the silent pleasures of his ways
are left bereft and mutely asking now
where shall we go to fill the magic show?

Albert knew his art and loved his ways
and thrilled the silver faces of the crowd
so much can one man do and go to rest
crowned in memories time cannot destroy.

At last these piercing shafts of lovely light
that empty stage that sees yet never knows

must always ring le bas when laughter joins
the art of making children of our hearts.

By Peter Mooney

Albert's ambition was to magically conquer the world with his own brand of magic by travelling to all four corners. All the research seems to confirm this was his aim, and he did at least achieve one ambition and that was appearing in America. Full details on this story will emerge later, but deep-down Albert was a family man. His wife and family came first, second, third and fourth – above everything else. Wherever he appeared in Ireland, he made sure he was back home that night giving them their rightful security. His story is a very special and fascinating one, and even after some slight delving into the magical past, it is also a unique one. It is only right and proper that his daughters tell his story from their unique perspective, and a very moving story it is too. So here I am, handing you, the reader, over to Barbara.

Chris

SCENE 1

--- ⚬⚬⚬ ---

Overture and Beginners

Mount Bellew is a quiet market town in County Galway in the west of Ireland.

It is surrounded by dappled paddocks and winding lanes bordered by stone walls with wild green hedges, all neatly tucked into the flowing folds of the Shiven river.

It was there on a cold January day in 1928 that thirty-two-year-old Josephine le Bas gave birth to her second child. A brother for five-year-old Ronald and another son for her beloved husband Samuel.

The proud parents called their child Albert Michael Terance le Bas.

As names go, there were few surprises as the le Bas family tree going back to 1574 is sprinkled with Alberts and Samuels in every generation. But perhaps this Albert was not only named for Samuel's own father, also Albert, but also to honour Samuel's younger brother another Albert. Thirteen years earlier at the tender age of twenty-three, he had lost his life on the battlefields of France, a mere twelve months after his only other brother, Leo aged twenty, had also died fighting under a French sky. It was a bittersweet legacy.

In 1928, Samuel le Bas who hailed from Dublin, was the bank manager of the Bank of Ireland in Mount Bellew, an astute businessman and a respected member of the local community. There was much merriment in their home 'Woodview' that day. As a young man, Samuel too had experienced fighting in the Great War and his experiences coupled with the loss of his only two brothers meant that he was a man carrying a heavy emotional burden. Sadly, this would play out in the

1

life of the new baby. But at that moment in time, on January 29th, 1928, this was a happy family.

This was the day Albert le Bas entered the world with curly white blond hair and soft smiling eyes. Little could he have known the opportunities, the challenges and the enormous highs and desperate lows that his short life would gift him.

As his father Samuel and all le Bas generations before him were Church of Ireland, being of Huguenot descent, you may assume that the baby Albert would also be of this faith (and indeed this misconception in later years afforded many contacts and opportunities, but that is for later in the tale). But this was not so.

When Samuel and Josephine Murphy married on Valentine Day in 1922 along with his marriage vows, Samuel promised, as was required at the time with 'mixed marriages' in a ferociously and predominantly Catholic Ireland, that any offspring of the marriage would be raised as Catholic. Albert did not follow his father to his alma mater, the Kings Hospital School in Dublin. Albert was baptised, received communion and was confirmed into the Catholic faith. An early glimpse into Albert's later life might be the fact that he took Leopold as his Confirmation name – not because he held any special devotion to the Patron Saint of Austria but instead because Leopold was the name of Harry Houdini's brother. Yes, it was also his uncle's name, but I quite like the Houdini connection too.

Early days are hard to track for this little family. Over the years, Samuel was posted to several Bank of Ireland branches around the country, as was the custom at the time. This meant the family relocated and the boys changed schools' multiple times. Samuel's own mother Bridget had passed away when he was just thirteen years old and when he was seventeen, his father remarried a lady called Henrietta. Family stories would indicate that Samuel's relationship with his father was strained and more so after committing the unforgivable crime of marriage to a Catholic in 1922. Despite this, young Albert did spend many a happy carefree holiday visiting either his mother's family who hailed from Kilkenny or with his colourful grandfather Albert le Bas.

His grandfather Albert le Bas, as was the family tradition for generations, was the Irish Assay Master in charge of all the gold and silver in and out of Ireland. He was also a smart businessman who had accumulated a vast property portfolio, not least a row of Georgian houses in Rathgar – appropriately named Le Bas Terrace, and a selection of properties on Leeson Street in Dublin, plus a beautiful lakeside property in Lough Dan in County Wicklow. This retreat in County Wicklow is known locally as the 'Le Bas House' and many a summer was spent there by young Albert and his brother.

In later years, Albert and Betty both stayed in Lough Dan with Albert's grandmother. Betty used to say that despite the beautiful surroundings, evening times at Lough Dan were a nightmare as 'the midges would eat you alive!'. Over the years, I have visited the property and it is truly a beautiful piece of lush green Irish countryside. Many years later, in my great grandfather's will, he donated the property in Lough Dan to the Boy Scouts of Ireland who still use it as an adventure campground today.

But I digress.

The five-year gap between Ronald and Albert meant that when Albert was only seven, his brother and playmate Ronald left for the Jesuit boarding school in Mungret College, County Limerick, leaving Albert alone for months at a time.

Were these the times when he first amused himself with a box of tricks he received as a present when he was seven? It was 1935. Irish Magician Hubert Lambert wrote of Alberts's early life in the June 1950 edition of *The Linking Ring*. He wrote, "He was flabbergasted with the peculiar peregrinations of four corks under a hat, shown to him by his cousin, and thus felt the first tentative nibble of that incurable virus, the magic bug."

Was this when his love for the ancient craft of magic first fascinated him and ignited a passion in his boyish heart that would last a lifetime? I would like to think so. The truth may be a bit sadder.

It was more likely there was a need for a hobby, a refuge and a desperate attempt by a young child to find a happy place where people around you would laugh and only imagined things could possibly become real. A childish ploy to provide distraction and unity.

As the years progressed, a change had come over his father Samuel. Buried memories of his time at war began to surface. Initially, perhaps as fleeting uninvited thoughts and occasional nightmares but these progressed like an ever-shifting fog to the terrible reliving of the stink of the trenches, the feel of mud, cold and hunger, the memories of rats and dead comrades – images that were burnt in his brain and could not be unseen, the loss of his only brothers and the guilt of being sent home as the last of the family's sons. This bubbling cauldron of distress began to fester inside Samuel and gradually raised its ugly head.

In today's world, we understand the term Post Traumatic Stress Disorder or PTSD. We understand and can treat the symptoms. We appreciate the terrible impact of vicarious trauma and validate the feelings of those affected. In those days, it was described as 'shell shock' – a movement of the brain allegedly caused by being close to an explosion. Even if they were not in the vicinity of shell fire, soldiers came home with tangled and misunderstood emotions. There was little understanding and less sympathy and so, the smart thing to do was to deny those emotions, hide the symptoms and pretend you were ok. Keep them to yourself, carry on and be productive in a job that would give you a sense of achievement and a means to support your family – like a respectable career in banking.

There was no help, not that the shame of it would prompt you to seek help anyway. Ex-soldiers like Samuel found other less efficient and ultimately more self-destructive coping strategies. For Samuel, he sometimes found escape from his troubling thoughts and nightmares in the clear amber elixir that was Irish whiskey.

Despite the many moves around the country, Albert and his family were constant visitors to their relatives in Dublin and spent the holidays in the family summer place in Bettystown, County Meath. It was during one of these holidays in the summer of 1938 that the then ten-year-old Albert took to the public stage for the first time. It was a variety show in the local school and Albert appeared using the nom-de-theatre *Prince Puzzlem Wonder Boy Magician*. This successful 'first blood' led to a series of engagements in schools throughout the country. So, his career was off to a flying start. He spent every penny of his pocket money on tricks and his mum helped out by making exotic costumes befitting a 'prince'.

But all was not well on the home front.

By the time Albert was eleven, his father had resigned from the bank. Despite Josephine's attempts to help him, he felt he could no longer maintain a job, a marriage or a parental role. Little is known of the struggles and turmoil of this time. Was the disintegration of his functioning a rapid or a slow growth that young Albert witnessed but was helpless to do anything about? Who knows? There are some stories your parents do not tell you.

Samuel left the family.

On December 6th, 1939, Samuel left Ireland and took the boat to Liverpool.

In 1939, Europe was at war. Although Ireland, thanks to the determination of Eamon De Valera, was declared neutral, we were a European country and there was rationing. There were curfews and the 'glimmer man' would do his nightly rounds to ensure that streetlamps were extinguished. Most families had relatives who were part of the British Army and they were scared. This was wartime and as an Irish citizen, a travel permit was required between Ireland and England.

There is a photo of Samuel's travel permit. In it, at age forty-eight, Samuel looks like a much older and very broken man. It is easy to summarise this event in three lines for this book but the implications for the eleven-year-old Albert and sixteen-year-old Ronald must have been enormous. Ronald was still away at boarding school. Now without a husband and with no reason to be living in an unfamiliar country town, his mother took herself and Albert back to the shelter of her own family in County Kilkenny.

Albert's mother Josephine Murphy had come from a respected and prosperous family in County Kilkenny. Her father was a successful businessman who owned Murphy's pub on the High Street, the local jewellers and a couple of tobacconist shops. It was to her sister's house that Josephine took her young sons. Her sister Cissy had married a gentleman by the name of Bourke, a widower with six children. They had six more children together and they were raising their large family in their grand house called Seville Lodge. It was here Albert spent the next period of his life playing with his cousins. For a short time, he attended the local school and spent time with the family's two giant Irish Wolfhounds.

Samuel did not completely desert his family. In England he was working and sending money back to Josephine. Enough for her to live independently and by the age of thirteen, Albert and his mother were back in their native Dublin. Back in Rathgar, not far from where the le Bas family had always lived, and where Samuel had been reared. They settled in a Georgian house in Grosvenor Road, Rathgar.

Albert's grandfather, also Albert, passed away in April 1941 and so he lost another male role model. Interestingly, there is no record of Samuel, his son, returning to Ireland that year to bury his father – perhaps their relationship had ended with Samuel's departure in 1939, or the rift from his marriage to a Catholic woman was so vast, it was uncrossable. It is an unsolved mystery.

In Rathgar, the curly-haired Albert continued taking his first tentative steps into the world of entertainment. During holidays, his brother Ronald joined him in his shows and Ronald himself became very professional with a Punch and Judy Show. In one of Albert's ledgers – handwritten in faded blue fountain pen, there is an account of a variety show in which he performed on Tuesday 21st, December 1941 at The Army Portobello Barracks in Dublin. He recorded his act as four tricks: The Cut and Restored Hankie, Colour Changing Cards, Bag Trick and finishing with The Hat Trick. His assistant was Ronnie and his comments on the performance were:

> *Appeared in everyday clothes - short pants. The fake for the cut and restored hankie slipped as I entered and so I had to scrap that trick. I think the table was too high, so people could not fully see the corks for the Hat Trick. About 500 people present.*

These ledgers are a record he kept of all his young performances – by the age of fifteen he had written details of fifty-five appearances, including a concert in Mornington, County Meath on July 26th, 1942. In his ledger he remarks:

> *Appeared in Eastern costume with a little beard, no mishaps - appeared for the first time as Prince Puzzlem.*

And so, for Albert Michael Terance Leopold le Bas, the story of his lifetime love affair with the magical world begins. A world full of famous conjurers, suspended disbelief, laughter and illusion, grease paint and sparkles but mostly, a world of happiness and friends.

Along the way, this magical arena in which my parents played, afforded us children an exceptionally privileged lifestyle and a childhood that was so rich and diverse that it is sometimes hard to describe.

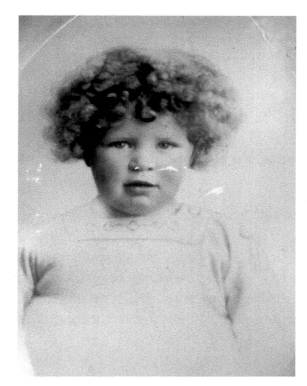

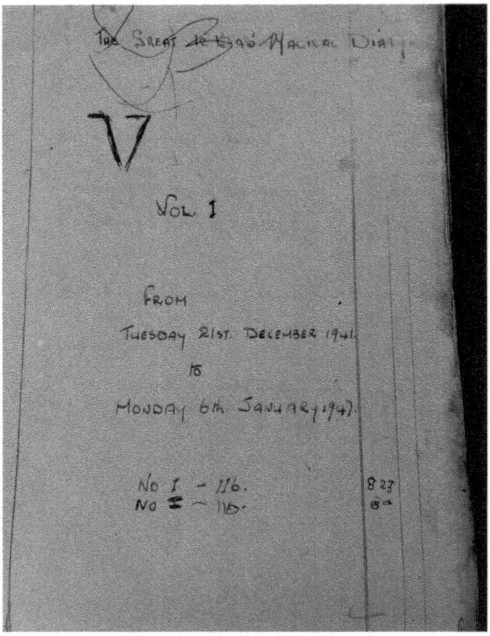

The Great le Bas' Magical Diary

V

Vol. 1

From

Tuesday 21st. December 1941.

to

Monday 6th January 1947.

No I – 116.

No II – 110.

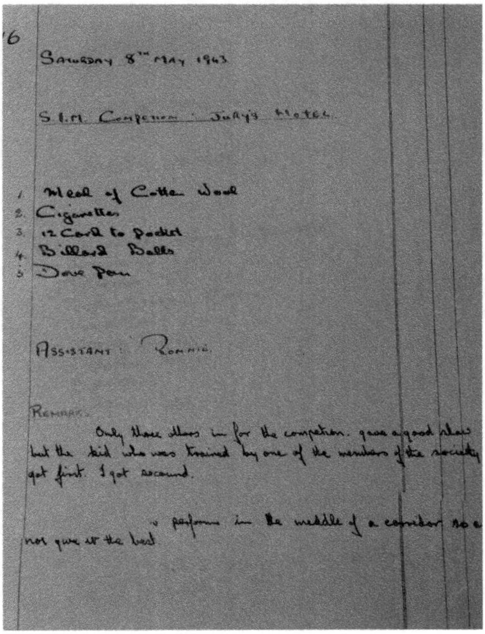

6

Saturday 8th May 1943

S.I.M. Competition · Jury's Hotel

1. Meal of Cotton Wool
2. Cigarettes
3. 12 Card to Pocket
4. Billiard Balls
5. Dove Pan

Assistant: Rommie

Remarks

Only three others in for the competition. gave a good show but the kid who was trained by one of the members of the society got first. I got second.

perform in the middle of a corridor so not give it the best

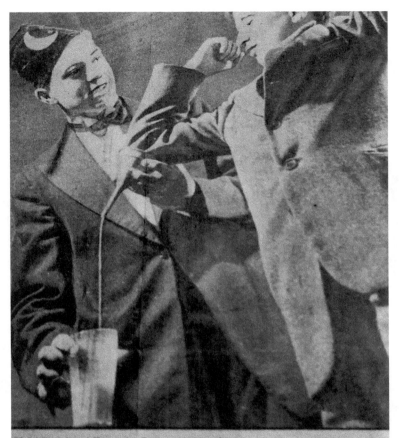

SMAN Mr. Albert le Bas, turning his attention to the mechar
g's most spectacular performance. He places a jug of mil
his arm and—presto! How is it done? That remains Mr. le

SCENE 2

Magician in Training

During the 1940s, life settled into a secure routine for Albert and his mother. Ronald was continuing his education in Mungret College and Albert was happily in school in Terenure College. These were the war years, or as we called it in Ireland 'The Emergency', and items such as white flour and oranges were a distant memory for many. Although officially neutral, Ireland was bombed. On January 2nd, 1941, German bombs were dropped on Terenure, the neighbouring suburb to Rathgar. The following morning there was further bombing of the South Circular Road, again not too far from Albert's home. There were injuries but thankfully no deaths. This must have been a scary time for all. Later that year in May, four German bombs fell on the northside of Dublin killing twenty-eight people.

It is hard to imagine this being a time for frivolity but in fact, there were quiet strides being taken in the world of entertainment. The Theatre Royal in Dublin had opened its doors in 1935. During the war years, they embraced a hybrid entertainment form known as 'cine-variety' whereby a variety stage show, and a film were all included in the price of a ticket. The Theatre Royal's offering to its patrons was an electric theatre organ (a Compton), some dancing girls and a film. This format, also adopted by other cinemas, would go on to provide a launch pad for some great local and international variety performers.

In 1941, Albert performed at the Crumlin Carnival and was billed as *Ali Pasha*. The carnival flyer announced: 'You must see Ali Pasha, Grand Wonder Show! First time to Ireland! New! Mysterious! Fantastic!'

Young Albert had his eye on a bigger audience than schoolchildren and carnival-goers. In November 1942, he entered a talent contest in the Queen's Theatre in Dublin. With Ronald as his assistant, they performed a show they had received a good reception to in the past. The tricks were: The Cut and Restored Hankie, Soup Plate, Colour Changing Cards, The Dice Box and the Telephone Directory Illusion. Sadly, there is no record of how they went in that particular talent contest, but Queen's Theatre producer Paddy Grogan arranged that Albert would be a guest artist for a week in December. Following on from that engagement, Le Bas and Company in *Mighty Magic* topped Paddy's bill on many occasions.

In February 1945 at the Society of Irish Magicians (SIM) Young Conjurer Competition held in Jurys Hotel in Dublin, Albert gave a performance consisting of: Meal of Cotton Wool, Fan Cards, 30 Card Trick, Coin Production and Restored Paper. He did not win but came second. His ledger entry for that show was as follows:

Gave a good show, but the kid trained by the president of the society got first. How he got it is obvious. There were eleven contestants. It lasted from four o'clock until nine o'clock. I got second.

This effort may not have won him the prize that year but what it did give him was his first picture and mention in a national newspaper. An article in the Dublin Evening Mail with the alluring caption 'Boy Produces Iced Cake from Empty Saucepan' reported on the competition as follows:

In a small upstairs room in Jurys Hotel on Saturday evening 10 boys whose ages ranged from 13 to 16, competed for a shield presented by the Society of Irish Magicians for the best juvenile conjurer. This was the second competition held by the society for the purpose of encouraging young magicians. The winner keeps the shamrock shaped shield and each entrant receives a prize and is made an associate member of the society. A novel idea was introduced this year a special prize being awarded to whoever spoke his 'patter' in Irish. Mr Sean O'hUadhaigh judged the Irish and Dr C. H. Denham judged the conjuring. The boys performed on a small stage at one end of the room and were each allowed approximately 15 minutes in which to mystify the audience. They all showed great confidence and carried out their tricks in great style… Last year's winner was again successful. He is John Hollingsworth, 31 Hollybank Avenue Ranelagh, and is at present being trained by Mr Chaney… Domhnall O'Siogfrada won the prize for patter in Irish. Second prize for conjuring went to Albert le Bas, 64 Grosvenor Road, Rathgar who had some very amusing patter and good sleight of hand. The other competitors were Alan Brown, Charles McSherry, Thomas Gibson, Rodney Gilbert, Victor Armstrong, David Eustace and Gerard Moore. The latter's final trick was appreciated by the ladies in the audience he produced an iced cake from what appeared to be an empty saucepan.

By day, Albert attended school at Terenure College and by night paying little attention to homework, immersed himself in magical books and began his lifelong habit of practice, practice, practice. He got publicity cards printed, acquired a new more mysterious costume, joined the international *Brotherhood of Magicians – British Ring* and subscribed to any international magic publications he could.

As the 1940s progressed, he got himself a Saturday job with a company called *Gings* on Dame Street, Dublin. They were suppliers of theatrical costumes and novelty items. Albert's job was as an errand boy, delivering orders around Dublin on his bicycle. No prizes for guessing where all his money went. He continued to be close to his mother, making sure he had tea with her every day and bringing her to many concerts and shows.

He changed schools for the final years of his education to Belvedere College. He was quietly making a name for himself in Dublin and beyond, and his picture and write ups were now appearing with regularity in the newspapers. His mother was proud of him and I believe his father was too, albeit somewhat silently. His father returned home in 1946 and 1947 for short stays. Albert was desperate to maintain contact with him and sought out opportunities to visit the UK for magical shows or conventions during these years. At home he had his magic, his job and when time afforded it, his social life. Over the years, both himself and Ronald had always taken their mother on a European holiday each summer. Albert spent lazy Sunday afternoons at the beach with his pals, sporting hilarious crimplene swimming trunks!

Amongst the hundreds of appearances throughout the 1940s, Albert changed stage names a few times. On February 3rd, 1946, he appeared at the Royal Dublin Society (RDS) as part of a lecture program by CF Hollingshead 'Magic Yesterday, Today and Tomorrow'. He was assisted by AJ Palmer and Neil Phelan and now calling himself *Vandini* he performed The Great Escape. In this he escaped from a padlocked sack on stage only to appear at the end of the hall.

A little later in April 1946, his ledger has commentary on a show in Fosters Hall in Delgany, County Wicklow with his friend Frank as his assistant. It gives some insight into the challenges of a young magician. He writes:

Frank met me at Mount Street. There we met Patterson and then went on the train to Greystones. We had tea in Patterson's house and we got from Patterson's house to Delgany in his Dodge. Everything was ready. Frank was on stage with the tray for Fire Eating. I was announced - the music started, the curtain went up and - I blew the mains! So, I carried on in the dark, that was alright for the Fire Eating but what next? I turned into a comedian for half an hour in the dark. The ESB (Electricity Supply Board) electrician had to be sent for. Otherwise the show went OK. The Milk Trick got them. I appeared in costume.

This Milk Trick was obviously a favourite and a crowd pleaser as Albert also used it again on April 13th, 1946 as a performer at the Society of Irish Magicians (SIM) 1946 convention in Jurys Hotel. His act on that occasion was recorded as: Invisible Dog, Production of Fans, Card Manipulations, 12 Cards to Pocket, 30 Card Trick, Coin Production and Milk. His comments were:

Show went terrific! The Milk got them!

Gone were the costumes, the Eastern Magician or ancient Wizard, he wrote:

Appeared in dinner jacket and fez.

An authentic red wool fez that soon, along with his chosen magic words 'Gilly Gilly' and a sprinkle of 'Oofle Dust' (his secret invisible magic dust) would become his trademarks for many years to come.

A huge advantage for this eighteen-year-old boy was of course the income he was earning from all his appearances. For example, a children's party in the ballroom of the Gresham Hotel in May 1946 had a huge list of tricks, starting with Fire Eating moving on to The Chinese Rings, Thumb Tie, Rattle Box, Dice Box, 30 Card Tricks, Cut and Restored Rope and ending in Coin Production. His audience was about eighty kids and twenty adults. His fee for the afternoon was three pounds thirty pence. Not a bad income for a schoolboy.

By June 1946 aged eighteen, Albert had finished his Leaving Certificate in Belvedere College with not too shabby a result. In hindsight, this was a significant milestone as records show that up to 1957 only 10,000 Irish students had achieved this level of education and sat the Leaving Certificate Examination. Albert scored himself a job as a car salesman with RW Archer, the main Ford dealer in Ireland. He had the patter and enough recognition to be able to negotiate good terms that would allow him some flexibility to work around his magical career. For their part, Archers' were getting an enthusiastic young gun who was honest, reliable, good with customers and whose name was becoming increasingly known. It was a win-win arrangement. He was based in Sandwich Street, Dublin which was not too far to travel home for lunch each day with his mother in Rathgar. Albert was to remain working with Archers in various roles for all of his non-magic working career.

At the age of nineteen, Albert joined the famous Abbey Theatre Company and was the first performer to show magic on their hallowed stage. This was open sesame to the lucrative series of engagements in circles hitherto closed, leading to a broadening in his vista of the potential of magic.

Chris writes: 'Abracadabra' are the famous magic words known the world over, but *Abracadabra* or *Abra* as it was affectionately known, was the world's only magical weekly magazine. A magic magazine that from its first issue in February 1946, it appeared every week and ran for some sixty-three years totalling some 3,296 issues. Each Friday, it would be dutifully posted and the following morning without fail it would appear through your letterbox as if by magic. Ah, those were the days. Even with postal and printers strikes it was never ever late – the editor saw to that! *Abra* arrived with all the latest topical and magical news from around the world and was lovingly run by a wonderful

Barbara le Bas

warm-hearted man called Charles Goodliffe Neale. He lived in Birmingham and ran a successful church furnishing business and was known worldwide simply by the name of Goodliffe. To highlight how appreciated he was, he received a Papal Knighthood for his services to the Catholic Church. He travelled the world on business and also as a wonderful magical ambassador and in so doing created a society called the 'Fellowship of the Flying Sorcerers'. Sadly, he would be struck down later in life with multiple sclerosis but that certainly didn't stop him travelling! It is rather spooky that the first mention of a young Albert was in that very first volume of *Abra* where, on page 12, there was a report on the All Ireland Magic Convention on April 13th, 1946.

The reviewer, Neil Phelan stated inter alia: "Albert Le Bas (*Vandini*) only recently up from the Junior Section showed promise of becoming one of Ireland's foremost performers. Opening with his 'Invisible Dog' effect he performed an act full of wisecracks and humour and fooled all the magicians with his thirty cards and Cards up the Sleeve."

Volume 2 and the December 21st issue #47 of the Society of Irish Magicians reports that: "At our last meeting we had Chris Charlton (who had been appearing at the Olympia), his charming wife and daughter as our guests. With dinner over, magic followed with Albert le Bas, Neil Phelan, and Diana all doing slick close-up. Suffice to say that it was the early morning when the meeting broke up."

It might just be worth mentioning at this point that a lot of references to gatherings of magicians not just in Ireland but internationally, tend to end with the words 'it was the early morning before we left', 'it was a late night all around' or words to this effect. Albert was a teetotaller all his life, and I understand that when a meeting or a chance encounter with another magician carried on into the wee hours, it was actually fuelled by passion and not alcohol!

Issue #97 goes on to mention that at the recent AGM Albert had been elected Treasurer of the SIM. Albert was slowly climbing the ladder. Still with *Abra* – by issue #103 it was now December 1948 and it reported that another well-known performer, Ali Bey, who had also appeared at the nearby Olympia theatre was similarly fêted by the SIM. Albert allegedly said, "I have always said that if you mix with professionals long enough then some of it has to rub off." Albert had started well, for both Charlton and Bey were exceptional well-travelled magicians and fine entertainers. Issue #194 details Goodliffe travelling to Dublin presumably on business, not only as Ireland was recognised, respected and known as a Catholic country but also in the knowledge that a warm welcome awaited anyone connected with magic. Along with others, Albert entertained Goodlife that night. From their first meeting, the bond of friendship grew and would last Albert's lifetime, as we will read later.

During the late 1940s, Albert continued to perform as much as possible, now with the added benefit of driving a company car (Ford), there was not an engagement he turned down or a county in Ireland that he did not visit. He trod the boards for local church concerts, charitable events and private parties. He was becoming quite popular as the entertainer of choice for the 'horsey crowd', making genuine friendships, many of which would be lifelong.

His performances were written up on a regular basis in national and local papers. Whenever possible during this time, Ronnie was still his assistant, as was a childhood friend Frank. Ronnie had developed a nice sideline for himself as a puppeteer, billed as Mr Benton. Together, the brothers had danced around the skirts of variety and private entertainment in Ireland. But Ronnie was grown up now. He had graduated from Mungret and joined the Irish Army.

Increasingly, Albert performed solo and began accumulating a large selection of illusions. As magic was becoming more and more an accepted segment in variety and the stages and platforms were getting bigger, the magic of close-up and legerdemain was no longer appropriate. For bigger stages, Albert needed bigger props and more spectacular illusions. He tested the waters outside of Ireland and performed in England and Spain many times at magical conventions but also at theatres and events that were not necessarily gigs obtained through the magical circles in which he moved.

In 1949, he signed a contact with the Queens Theatre – the venue of his talent contest attempt a few years previously. He was booked for their Summer show 'Roll Out the Laughs' from July 16th and for his work, he was paid the princely sum of fifteen pounds per week – which was probably three times his weekly wages with Archers. The stage names of *Prince Puzzelem* and *Ali Pasha* were in the past, he now billed as *Le Bas and Company*.

Chris writes: 1949 The International Brotherhood of Magicians is a US based magic organisation that had satellite societies in different parts of the world called a 'Ring'. Each month every member of the Ring would receive a sometimes 100-page magazine telling other fellow members what was going on around the world. This magazine was aptly called *The Linking Ring*. In the May issue of *The Linking Ring* Vol 29 No 3 page 94, there was an article by Hubert Lambert, someone who certainly had a brilliant way with words. Each time he caught the eye of the reader immediately, on this occasion with an alliterative title *Goblins Gambol at Grenore*.

"January 29th, 1949 will be a long-remembered day to the peace-loving citizens of Glenore in County Louth, Ireland, for 'twas that day the goblins invaded their town. From the hills they came from the valleys, the boreens, and boroughs of Wicklow, Meath, Down, Dublin, Kildare and Antrim. By iron horse and horseless carriage, these weird beings made their journey to this hitherto normal town of about 834 population." Later in the descriptive article as a participant, Albert received his rightful mention. "Albert Le Bas, a fellow with a fez and a fund of funiosities, captured the full attention of the audience from the moment he pranced on. His thimble routine is full of surprises with nobody more 'surprised' than himself. But the most hilarious episode is his fast-moving act of milking through the elbow of an innocent helper and this merry tit-bit was relished by everybody."

Clearly Albert was on his way up.

Later in 1949, in the August *Linking Ring* (Vol 29 No 6 p88) Hubert Lambert reported: "Albert Le Bas, whose name, in our opinion couldn't be improved on for magical purposes, has been working as 'Ali Pasha' in the Crumlin Carnival, with a colourful act which was highlighted by 'Sawing a Woman in Half'. The sawee, a newcomer to the company, and evidently an impressionable young lady, swooned after the second show. Fortunately, this occurred in the wings after the sawing, so there was no on-stage contretemps."

Three months later in his November article, Hubert added that "sun-tanned and soft-spoken, Albert Le Bas has just returned from a sojourn in sunny Spain. With his penchant for flamboyant garb, we find it difficult to decide who was probably more impressed during this visit, the *hidalgos* or the Hibernian. With Spain as the locale of next year's International Congress of Magicians, Albert will know 'all the answers' when the time comes to arrange that trip to Barcelona."

In January 1950, it was reported in *Abra* that 'Ireland's Cold Convention' or 'Wizardry Below Freezing' was held at an old-world house, the Northlands Hotel in Bettystown, north of Dublin. The reporter stated it was 'devoid of heat and few examples of modern plumbing'! That certainly didn't stop the registrants having a good time which was compensated by the warmth of the organisers. Harry Stanley, over from London, was one of the magical dealers and he was presented with a suitably inscribed Shillelagh as a memento of his visit. SIM stalwart, Hubert Lambert presented the Bullet Catch illusion which, is dangerous at the best of times – to say the least, but Hubert pulled it off admirably. Hubert was a wise man with great judgement and someone who recognised 'talent' when he saw it and would perhaps be Albert's closest magical friend and mentor in the years that followed.

In the gala show, it was reported that "Le Bas and Company brought their slick illusion act and here is an up and coming performer scoring heavily with effects as different as the Dolls House and the Note in Cigarette." Although not mentioned in the report, it was also Albert's 22nd birthday!

From being a junior member of the SIM, he had risen in a few years to be a council member and was also a leading member of the Irish Ring no 85 of the International Brotherhood of Magicians.

As if all the aforementioned was not enough, in January 1950 Albert opened the first magical shop in Ireland. Hubert Lambert wrote of this:

> Assisted by his brother Ronnie and David Eustace, Albert was now prepared to fill the needs of the magicians in Ireland from his emporium at Grosvenor Road. This was a much-needed development that is welcomed by the local gimmick goons.

Hubert Lambert was asked to officially open the shop and in a dispatch to the International Brotherhood of Magicians he wrote:

> Remember some time back we mentioned that the le Bas brothers, Albert and Ronnie, were hard at work on a new magical shop? Well, the establishment is now in successful being, and thereby hangs a tale. Your scribe was asked to officially open the place, and on the appointed night a bevy of the local magicians assembled at the le Bas residence. Maps had been mailed to all, and the motley gathering proceeded en-masse to the new *Druids Den*!
>
> The gate to the street having been opened by the brothers, in we trooped to the foyer. This was brightly lit with coloured lights, and we were most impressed by the pillared entrance to the store, which was impeded by a white ribbon.

In the bubbling-with-excitement assembly were representatives of some of all the Irish Magical societies, including 'Doc' Denham (SIM), Tommy Murray (Mystic Circle) and Dan McAlister (Ulster Society of Magicians.)

A pair of scissors was thrust into our hand and the ceremony was on!

Seldom at a loss of words, we found it the easiest thing in the world 'to say a few words' on this very special occasion. 'Proud and pleased' came readily to the lips, and we knew we were merely voicing the thoughts of all those present. Each representative added his word of praise and encouragement, and then snip went the scissors, down went the ribbon, and "Now restore it!" went the boys!

At the last-minute Albert and Ronnie had disappeared. Suddenly the curtains between the pillars drew aside and before us was *The Druids Den* in all its glory, with the brothers behind the counter, jocularly rubbing hands in the well-known money-grabbers' fashion! They quickly however made it clear that this was strictly a social affair and then sprung a wonderful surprise on yours truly.

Speaking on behalf of himself and the 'general manager', Ronnie presented this Leprechaun with a magic wand engraved 'Presented to Hubert Lambert on the occasion of the opening of *The Druids Den*.' For once we were at a loss. This shall be a treasured possession. Right away, the two sparkplugs were hopping about among their guests serving refreshments, solid and liquid, and we were off on a really enjoyable night. Everybody did something magical. Oldies were trotted out; new ones given a first trial, favourites called for, and one lad 'Wolf-decked' his way around.

Hours later, we reluctantly went our respective ways, happy in the ways that we have been instrumental in giving *The Druids Den* a flying start. Since then, we have been over there many times. There is always something doing. One night for instance we dodged along to find there was a magic film showing. We had some fun that night! Ronnie kept hollering each time some prop came on the screen: "We've got that one in stock!"

By the end of the year, *The Linking Ring* Magazine was writing of magical things in Ireland. "'See you in le Bas's!' is the current chant over here right now, and an evening spent in the brother's shop is never ill-spent. Tuesdays and Fridays are shop nights and it is impossible to predict what weird personage will be among those present. Even Ronnie le Bas, who revels in the self-applied appellation, 'magicians mate' has been seen to pull off minor miracles."

Chris writes of this event: This piece appeared in the international magical magazine *The Linking Ring* in January 1950 (Vol 29 No 11, p98):

Albert wasn't just a talented artist, he could often see a business potential too. He approached Davenports of London the famous magical dealers who have been established since 1898 and still going today! They promptly appointed him as their Irish Agent. This was good news indeed for all Dublin's wand-wielders at that time as their city was not graced by any magical emporium at all.

Still living at 64 Grosvenor Road Rathgar Dublin, he opened his soon-to-become famous magical watering hole 'The

Druids Den', "Ireland's Only Magic Shop' offering 'The Latest in Magic' and he also issued an infrequent magazine called *The Druid* with the strapline 'If It's Good We Have It!'

1950 May, Albert reported that he had distributed copies of the magazine to his *The Druids Den* members. The National Association of Magical Societies held their annual convention in Dublin at the Gresham Hotel on O'Connell Street, Dublin. Once again, Albert closed the gala show with a first-rate act whose antigravity conjuring was conjuring of a very high order and whose happy presence won him immediate favour with the audience.

Albert was busy. It was recorded that in February 1950, he had been retained for no fewer than thirty-five banquets! It has been speculated as to how it was humanly possible to keep to the schedule, but he did. The evenings he spent on stage, accepting the accolades and delighting audiences were balanced with the odd stolen night for himself, when he went out with his non-magic friends and just enjoyed himself.

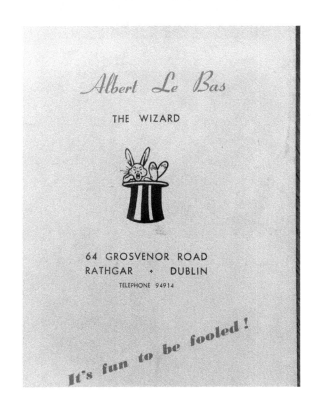

QUEEN'S THEATRE, DUBLIN

Date as Postmark

TALENT CONTEST

Your application for an Audition has been received, please attend at the Theatre on

......Wednesday, 11th Nov., '42.....................

at 10.30 a.m.

All Competitors using music **must provide their own**, otherwise it will not be possible to have an audition.

Signed **P. R. GOGAN,**

Manager

Albert Le Bas

THE WIZARD

64 GROSVENOR ROAD
RATHGAR • DUBLIN
TELEPHONE 94914

It's fun to be fooled!

SCENE 3

Making Waves

L ooking back at Ireland in the 1950s through the lens of twenty-first century technology, political correctness and instant communication, it is difficult today to truly appreciate what a restricted society it was.

The Catholic Church was a major influence on all aspects of life.

Politically, there were remnants of the civil war still in positions of power and economically, the decade has often been referred to in history books as 'The Lost Decade'. But the notions of stagnation, crisis or despair in Ireland during this era were erroneous.

It was a decade of explosion in the arts and theatre world with new works from Samuel Beckett, Patrick Kavanagh and Brendan Behan.

The Irish runner Ronnie Delaney won Gold at the 1956 Melbourne Olympics, putting Ireland on the world sporting map. There were signs that the politics of old were exhausted and censorship was beginning to lose its potency as traditional ideas and values were increasingly challenged. There was even talk of Ireland developing its own television industry.

The up and coming generation of educated and employed men and women were starting to flex their muscles, push the boundaries and enjoy themselves away from the watchful eye of the local parish priest. Dance halls were booming. People were swinging to the sounds of the big bands and movie goers were enthralled by sexy sirens like Marilyn Monroe.

In 1950, Albert and Elizabeth met at a dance in Mount Pleasant Tennis Club in Ranelagh which is a suburb equidistant to both Rathgar where Albert lived and Donnybrook where Betty lived. Albert and Betty were both just twenty-two years old. That year had been an eventful one. Albert's father Samuel had returned home for the last time from the UK and was living in the family home in Rathgar, and so to all intents and purpose, Albert was again living with both parents. Betty had danced in Mount Pleasant with her friends many times and at the end of the night they would all usually get a lift home from an older gentleman called Eddie Collins, a bachelor pharmacist who just loved to dance and would turn up at every local dance with his smart suit and polished shoes, and just for the joy of it, he would dance with nearly all the young ladies. They all knew and liked him. He was a nifty dancer. An extra bonus was of course, that he had a car for the trip home.

On this particular night, Betty was dressed in the dress she had made for her 21st birthday party in the Metropole Ballroom – pale blue off the shoulder moiré taffeta with a nipped in waist. Albert was not a dancer but somehow, he inveigled the slim and pretty Betty Merriman to dance with him all night. Years later when Betty was old, she would talk fondly of that first night, with a glow in her eyes and remember that she was struck by Albert's gentleness and manners but hastened to add that the main attraction that evening was the predicament that Eddie Collins was not there, and Albert conveniently enough, happened to be a man with a car!

From Albert's perspective, he was smitten from the minute he first saw her – and what was not to like? Betty Merriman was tall, slim, dark haired with deep set eyes and high cheekbones. She was smart, shy but assertive and Albert decided from that very first night she would be the woman he would marry and share his life with.

Over the years, I have come to appreciate that for both of them, shared values were important. Both were seeking not only love but an enduring relationship. They wanted what neither of their parents had.

Within weeks they were dating regularly, they went to the movies on nights that Albert was not doing a show, usually the Stella Cinema in Rathmines. They visited the theatre and saw *Juno and the Paycock* in The Abbey and visiting entertainers including Abbott and Costello and Frankie Laine in the Theatre Royal.

As Betty fell hook, line and sinker for this enigmatic and driven man, it was inevitable that the world of magic became her world too. From early on, this relationship transformed her from a quiet accounts clerk to a dynamic confident woman who would, in time, strut her sexy legs in miniscule sequined stage costumes and by all accounts, she loved and revelled in every minute.

Within a short time, they became besotted with each other. They met each other's families and Albert made a lifelong connection with Betty's mother Mary Merriman and Betty's brothers Myles, the youngest, and Eddie, who sadly at that time was struggling with multiple sclerosis, and with her sister Nuala.

In turn, Betty was taken on a Sunday afternoon to meet Albert's mother in Grosvenor Road. A story often told to us as children was that they were nearing the house when it was discovered that Betty had forgotten her gloves and so they turned around and drove back to Donnybrook to get them. This may seem trivial today, but it gives us a glimpse into just how proper and respectful these young people were at that time. By all accounts, the meeting went well.

Perhaps it is not just in storybooks that you find that one person who compliments you so well they are literally your better half and without them you are incomplete and sad.

And of course, Betty joined the act and became the glamorous assistant. Her hairdresser appointments became more frequent and her on-stage costumes were now meticulously made by the Dublin dressmaker Mrs Caulfield. By day, she continued working in the accounts department of Hughes Brothers in Rathfarnham and by night she swapped the modest skirts and twin sets for high heels, black fishnet stockings and miniscule sequined strapless dresses. She loved learning the tricks and together they practiced the illusions for hours.

This was always one of Albert's strengths – patience. He would practice and practice. A new routine, gag or trick would not be seen in public until it was word and action perfect. It is interesting that in all available notes and diaries, in critiques or write ups, there is never a mention of a trick that fell flat or a gag that bombed. Along with practice, he had an eerie knack with timing and so, as he performed more and more, now with his beautiful assistant, the patter became more polished and the routines flowed flawlessly.

This increasingly glamorous couple made plans for a life together, the house that they would make a home, the children, the holidays, the ongoing pursuit of recognition and achievement in the field of magic. They wove their dreams together and imagined a world of international opportunities, of excellence and recognition in the world of entertainment and all the while, of building a safe happy and secure family environment to come home to. These were achievable dreams in the 1950s in Ireland, there was a buzz and a change in the air, not only in the world of entertainment but in prospects generally.

The entertainment scene was changing. There was the possibility of television, of cheaper travel and international fame. Albert had already completed a summer season in the south of France and had performed many times in the UK. His name was out there, and he was driven. He wanted it all and he wanted the beautiful Betty at his side. But this was 1950s Ireland and an integral part of their relationship and future plans was grounded in their faith. As dusk fell one spring evening in 1951 in the quiet church of St Theresa's on Clarendon Street, Dublin, together they knelt before the main alter, and in the warm glow of the votive candles, Albert proposed. A proposal Betty readily accepted.

May 1951 marked another milestone for Albert. The world of television beckoned invitingly. Television was first received in Ireland in 1949 following the opening of high-power BBC transmitters at Sutton

Coldfield near Birmingham, giving marginal reception along parts of the east coast. Of course, only a handful of people had television sets and for the general population, radio was the main vehicle for entertainment in the home. The first transmissions on the island of Ireland began with the launch of BBC Northern Ireland in 1953 and later, the launch of Ulster Television (UTV) in 1959.

Throughout the 1950s, the government of Ireland were worried about the influences of British television and the popularity of the medium. By the end of the 1950s, 60% of the population could receive BBC1 and the UK ITV channels. The Irish government began to discuss the provision of an Irish television service, a discussion headed up by Leon Ó Broin, the secretary at the Department of Posts & Telegraphs, who had responsibility for Radio Eireann, Ireland's radio service. In 1950, Ó Broin established his own committee on Irish television and bought a television set to receive broadcasts from the BBC. The department of finance were worried at the cost of setting up a new television service and dismissed the possibility on several occasions during the 1950s.

However, one of the main attractions of the annual Royal Dublin Society Spring Show in Ballsbridge in Dublin in May 1951 was the Television Tent – an example of what home-produced television entertainment would look like. The occasion was written up in the Dublin Evening Mail newspaper:

> Heavy rain kept the crowds indoors on the second day of the Spring Show in the RDS grounds. Television and the trade stands were the chief attractions for spectators. The television tent was a big attraction this morning the only drawback being that the people had to queue up in the rain between shows. If ever television does come permanently to Ireland there need never be any fear that there will not be enough Irish talent to keep up entertaining programmes. Viewers today were able to see a very good miniature variety

show in which such artists such as Roy Croft and Albert le Bas, Magician took part.

This was the first home-produced broadcast example of Irish television. Of course, Albert was involved.

Later that day, Albert received a telegram from Mr Neil Phelan President, on behalf of the Society of Irish Magicians, it simply said: "Congratulations on your television show excellence." A telegram he kept for years. It would be another ten years before Ireland did eventually launch their own television service.

Despite Albert's success in honing his craft and laying foundations for his magical career during this time, there were unsettling periods when Ireland felt too small and limited to the ambitious Albert. The motor car industry was well established and escalating in developing nations. In 1952, Albert turned his sights towards Eldoret in the Kenya Colony of East Africa where the Ford Motor Company were establishing themselves. The Kenya Colony had been a British Protectorate since 1920 and it was to a local motor car company, Hughes, that Albert wrote in March of 1952 submitting a job application. He received a positive reply later that month advising him: "While there is not all the scope that you may imagine for a motor car salesman in a place like Eldoret, there is however every scope for a general salesman in the car trade which would include the selling of accessories, spare parts, and parts from cars and tractors." The letter went on to state they were very interested in his application. They asked when was the earliest he could leave Ireland and what salary would he expect.

At the end of the day, one can only presume that between himself and Betty they decided that the better option was to continue working with Archers in Dublin, continue with his magical dreams and forget all about selling tractors in Africa. Just as well as later that year the Mau Mau conflict began in Kenya which was a long and bloody strike for independence that did not end until 1963. A lucky escape indeed.

Magically speaking, 1952 was again a busy year. A half page article in the *Times Pictorial Week* in February put the spotlight again on The Druids Den with the caption: *This Shop Is Closed to The Public.*

The journalist delightfully describes his visit: "Some people never grow up. They bring you out to tea and no sooner are you in a quiet side street, than you are pushed into a car, a bandage is put over your eyes and you are whisked away... The contact was quiet and courteous but there was no explanation for the ride. With all these stories of the NKVD and atom secrets and G-Men... Well, there was some reason for nervousness. But the reporter and photographer need not have worried, it was a gag of sorts. They brought us to a shop where the proprietor is very particular about his clients. You see he sells magic. Then the explanation came 'We have to be so careful, sorry for the scare. But we have to keep the whereabouts of this place secret. It could be so useful to lawless folk. We keep valuable documentation here. How to catch a bullet in the teeth, for example.'"

The reporter goes on to tell how Albert is of Huguenot descent while describing the production of multiple live goldfish appearing in an empty bowl and then their disappearance from the same bowl.

He writes: "But the act of the night is still to come, the sawing up of that very decorative young woman, Betty Merriman. Sawing people up is not nowadays permitted by the law – except on the stage of course. Albert had a new way of doing it, performed with permission of the inventor and with the exclusive right to use it. Poor Betty was put on a bare plank supported by chairs. Thin body 'stocks' were put on her and short pieces of dowelling fitted into the holes down the sides of the stocks. Then we examined the saw. Nice sharp teeth. Good pliable blade. Strong handle. We handed it back nervously. Nothing 'dummy' about that saw. 'Druid le Bas' began sawing. But for the noise of the saw's teeth eating through the dowelling, there is silence in the room. An atmosphere of... suspended animation... Poor Betty. The saw goes through the dowelling, passing through the body of a silent Betty. And not a scream from her. Not even a wincing. When the stocks are cut through, they are taken away. The saw is now below the body of this girl. Yet she is in one piece when she stands up! When we stumble over each other in our anxiety to examine the saw, we find it as solid as ever."

Write ups like this, complete with pictures, were meticulously kept by Betty and pasted into a giant scrapbook.

In March, every day after their day jobs, Albert and Betty performed two shows a night in the Olympia Theatre's production of 'Dr Crock and his Crackpots'. This was a popular variety show with singers, dancers Syd and Paul Kaye, High Speed Arabian Tumblers, The Three Minalex and the Olympia Theatre orchestra. The program for this show interestingly has a footnote: 'In the interest of public health this theatre is disinfected throughout with Jeyes Fluid.' Good to know!

That year, Albert brought his act to the Magicians Convention in Holyhead and as usual, enjoyed all the camaraderie of a few days spent with fellow sorcerers including the Irish lot – Neil Phelan, Neta Kelly and Dr D McAllister.

This year, he travelled without Betty to do a winter season in Switzerland, visiting the casinos at Montreux and St Moritz. He sent her postcards and love letters daily, items carefully kept in crinkly plastic wrappings forever by Betty.

He baffled his motor industry colleagues at the Motor Traders Dinner and completed a week of cabaret in the Royal Marine Hotel. By now, he had incorporated aspects into his act and patter that were ever to identify him, not least his famous magic words 'Gilly Gilly'.

He was winning at this magic thing, was deeply in love, making money and living his best life. But again in early 1953, strangely, their thoughts turned to starting a new life in a land of greater prospects and opportunities. They applied for visas to Canada. There is a letter from the Canadian Embassy advising Betty of the success in her application and listing possible boats that she could travel on. Once again, I am presuming that when all options were on the table, the final decision was to remain in Ireland and aim for the stars within more local constellations.

1953 brought more good times, such as the trip to the Isle of Man in August to attend yet another international convention. This time Albert and Betty and a host of Irish Magicians were photographed for the *Dublin Evening Mail* before leaving Dublin Airport. Albert, complete with striped butcher's apron, did a quick performance of the sawing Betty in half at the foot of the steps to the plane. In December that same year, Albert added yet another accolade to his list when he won the coveted Ulster Cup at the Magicians competition held in Jurys Hotel by the Irish Ring of the International Brotherhood of Magicians.

Following their engagement, Betty sported a lovely five-stone diamond ring, but it would remain the only ring on her left hand for another while. Being cautious, Albert and Betty set their wedding date for 1955. They set about saving and securing a deposit for the home in which they would live and raise a family. Meanwhile, they were together most evenings. They played Bridge with Albert's parents, a game Betty always said was not at all frivolous but rather very competitive. Not only did Albert fall for Betty, but also for her mother, Mary Merriman. Forever known as Granny Merriman to us, she took a special place in his heart and they were firm friends for ever. Betty joined the le Bas family in Bettystown for their annual holiday where they would swim or play golf during the day, eat scallion and brown bread sandwiches in the dusk as Granny le Bas was preparing dinner. Betty survived the midges on weekends in his grandmother's summer residence in Lough Dan. They both remained devoted Catholics and attended weekly mass and annual religious retreats with vigour. The year passed in a flurry of shows and plans, and soon it ticked over into 1954.

There is a write up in Hubert Lambert's column in *The Linking Ring* that details the Gaelic Gathering of the convention (of magicians) around this time in Northlands Hotel. In passing, Hubert mentions that with Albert in the driving seat and his pretty fiancé by his side, they visited Albert's parents at their summer residence en-route to the convention. This was a colonial style building in its own grounds situated about a mile from the convention's hotel. Hubert writes: "in passing this does highlight to me that there was never any 'side' to Albert. He never came over as something other than what he was, a down to earth family man that was blessed with a huge talent. Never a 'show off' just happy that he could share his talents on stage or on the cabaret floor and make his audience feel happy."

In the summer of 1954, Albert and Betty accepted an engagement for several weeks of a summer season at Red Island Holiday Camp. Albert's family had known the Quinn family for many years. In 1948, Eamonn Quinn the patriarch of the family and quite the entrepreneur, started construction on a family business of a holiday camp that offered a range of facilities typical of British holiday camps at the time. It had a beautiful location on the beach at Skerries, North County Dublin and had 250 rooms accommodating up to 500 people a week. Most of the guests came from England and Northern Ireland, with some from Ireland.

As part of the holiday program, there was a variety show in the theatre each night. Albert loved this season, not least because over the years he had become firm friends with Eamonn's son Feargal. Feargal was an astute businessman who later went on to launch the Superquinn supermarket chain in Ireland, become an internationally respected businessman, a politician and eventually, a Senator for the National University of Ireland constituency from 1993 to 2016. In fact, a story often recounted by Albert was of how Fergal and his lovely wife Denise became engaged in the back of Albert's car one evening. Sadly, Feargal Quinn died many years later in April 2019.

Back to 1954 and the summer season… Every evening after work from his day job in Archers, he met Betty and together, they drove to Skerries. The show started at 7.30pm they delivered a faultless performance every night and then drove back to Dublin. Mindful that they were now saving in earnest to buy a house, Albert had opted to be paid all in one lump sum at the end of the season and when that day arrived, they got many months' worth of payment in cash. They took it straight to the First National Building Society and deposited it as their down payment on a house.

Betty's diary from 1954 notes a year of house inspections and one nearly completed offer on a new home to be built house in Glenageary, County Dublin, which they eventually pulled out of. On Tuesday November 16th, 1954 they finally settled on their new house. They bought in St Albans Park, Ballsbridge. This was a 1930s red brick three-bedroomed house with a big walled back garden with mature fruit trees in a quiet street at the tail end of Aylesbury Road, Ballsbridge and adjacent to Sydney Parade train station.

Their house had the name 'Dungooley' which meant little to either of them, and it was soon abandoned for the number forty-nine. Either the original owners or the immediate previous owners, must have had some notions of grandeur because in the maid's room adjacent to the breakfast room, there was a configuration of bells connected to pull-bells in the upstairs bedrooms. I am sure that in 1954, Albert and Betty did not realise what a blessing it was that this call system had been disconnected! The house cost just over three thousand pounds. Betty often said that she cried the night they signed for the keys, fearing that they would never be able to repay the mortgage. Ever traditional, they did not spend one night in the house until they were married, but instead, they gradually bought furniture and made furnishings in readiness for the start of their married life together.

Betty was creative and had a passion for decorating, so she quickly set about making the house a home. She was a determined and thrifty woman who furnished the house with an eclectic collection of new, old and downright odd pieces. She developed a love of house auctions and so a lot of their original furniture was pre-loved, including the only three-piece sofa that was ever in our home – a huge rolled arm couch and chairs in cut red velvet bought at auction from the home of the novelist Neville Shute. He was an Englishman whose father was appointed head of the post office in Ireland and who himself had a role to play in the Easter Rising in 1916, but whose fame came with his novels. But back to the couch... initially made in a thick velvet red and gold fabric but in later years modernised by Betty under loose covers to fit with the décor of the time.

On May 10th, 1955, Albert le Bas and Elizabeth Merriman were married in the Sacred Heart Catholic Church in Donnybrook, County Dublin. This was Betty's parish church.

As was traditional at the time, she was 'given away' and walked up the aisle by a cousin of her father's, Mr Laurie McGrath, who took on the role as her own father had passed away in 1951. Her bridesmaid was her sister Nuala and Albert's best man was his brother Ronald.

If this book had been written before April 2011, you may be forgiven for assuming that when Catherine Middleton was planning her wedding to Prince William in London, she took a sneak peek at Betty Merriman's wedding dress made in 1955 because it is remarkably similar! Both brides looked beautiful on their special day. Betty wore her hair back with a net and pearl encrusted headdress, one which her daughter Yvonne and her granddaughter Alma would also wear with pride on their wedding days in the distant future.

The wedding breakfast was held in the Hotel Pierre in Dun Laoghaire and attended by family and friends. These included some very youthful looking magicians from Dublin such as Neville Wiltshire, Hubert Lambert and Eustace Malcolm.

Following the wedding, the radiant couple flew to London for their honeymoon. I have not checked, but I have a feeling that perhaps along with the usual romantic times of a honeymoon, there was probably a visit to the Magic Circle and a quick trip to Davenports!

Albert and Betty settled into married life with careful gusto. As a married woman in Ireland, Betty had to give up her job and take on the role of wife, homemaker and in time, mother. Their home was close to the train line at Sydney Parade Avenue, so Betty often spent the morning in Dublin city visiting Cleary's, Arnott's or Brown Thomas or buying fresh fruit and vegetables from the colourful traders in Moore Street. She also shopped at local shops. An easy walk away, at the end of Saint Alban's Park was a footbridge that spanned the railway track and delivered you into the grounds of the Queen of Peace Church on Merrion Road, and from there it was a couple of hundred yards to the local shops: Brown's the newsagent and post office, Findlater's the grocer, the chemist shop and across Merrion Road was the local buy-everything general store. This shop was called Tracey's but was always referred to in our house as 'Jim Ham'.

As the years turned over and Betty got her first car – a pale blue Hillman Imp with the engine power of a good sewing machine, she also shopped in the nearby Sandymount Green, in Fry's Grocery Shop. There the butter and cheese were cut to order with a wire and patted into shape with wooden paddles, and the dried goods were weighed in front of you before being wrapped in brown paper bags. This was where I stood as a small child, mesmerised as the money and the change were whisked to and from the accounts office high above the shop floor on an unbelievable network of pullies and brass containers.

But I digress once again, back to 1955…

They travelled in September of that year to the nineteenth annual IBM convention in Southport where Albert's performance was a hit and where he acquired yet more interesting and new tricks. Performances in front of an audience of critical magicians was always a tough gig. In October, Albert was featured on the front cover of Max Andrews' *Magic Magazine*, a monthly UK publication.

By the end of the year, Betty was pregnant and radiant. She visited Dr Kevin Feeney the gynaecologist – whose receptionist always introduced her as 'the young-looking Grace Kelly'! On July 26th, 1956 at 26 Upper Lesson Street, in the Leinster Private Nursing Home, she delivered a dark-haired baby girl whom they named Louise Ann le Bas, as July 26th was Saint Ann's Day. There were never parents more besotted with a child. Betty took to motherhood like a dream and their little family and cosy home was a refuge from the buzz and fast paced world of entertainment. Albert continued to work in his day job for Ford. As the world of cabaret and entertainment that was not traditionally focused, developed more in Ireland, he also took engagements several nights a week to perform. By invitation of the Magic Circle, they performed at the Festival Show in the Scala Theatre London. His performance was recorded as:

"Albert le Bas was again the right choice for the second spot in that the voluble patter and speed of his act were in telling contrast to Leslie Lester's silent performance, and he continued to capture and hold the attention of the audience as well as to maintain a constant accompaniment of laughter. Albert's rapid-fire presentation of the changing card brought spontaneous laughter right at the start and his gags with the bucket and coins kept it going whilst he got the utmost ounce out of the burnt ten-shilling note. This eventually turned up in the clip of a diamond garter which mysteriously appeared on the leg of his attractive partner. Then a snappy version of 'Trouble' and finally, the production of a vast number of silks from his inexhaustible silver tube giving way to a triple spray of flags and a large Union Jack. Nothing very new in the content of the act but what a joy it was to appreciate each night the timing of the patter to get the laughs and how well it was all put over."

Married life ticked over. They were living the dream. Betty need not have cried at night anymore over impossible mortgage repayments. He was very well known around town and beginning to be the go-to entertainer for any national or international events. He was beginning to raise his fees and famously, Lord Alfred Beit remarked about him: "I pay for my racehorses and my conjurer, Mr le Bas in guineas." Within a few months of Louise's birth, Betty was again back on stage in her tiny costumes and her lovely sister Nuala, still unmarried, was a more than willing babysitter.

Albert and Betty performed more than ever, his patter and craftmanship getting more and more polished and her costumes getting smaller and more daring. There was reference to her having the best legs in Dublin! Hilariously, there was also a 'command' from the Catholic Bishop of Cork in a telegram to Albert after a matinee performance in Cork City to not appear on that evening's scheduled show if his assistant was going to wear such a shocking and revealing costume. He considered it an affront to good Catholic values and a breach of common morality. In true le Bas fashion, the telegram was put in the bin and the show went on!

Write ups in the national papers continued and over a few days in March that year, he was featured several times as he had challenged the editor of the paper that he would predict the headlines of a day later in the week. His prediction was delivered in a sealed envelope early in the week and on Thursday the headline ran: "He was right!"

That year saw another big purchase for Albert. Determined to keep the crown of having the biggest collection of magical illusions in Ireland, and quietly feeding his passion for bigger challenges, to their absolute delight he managed to purchase a very special illusion from a lady called June McComb in Belfast. A magician in her own right, June McComb was also a former beauty queen and once held the Miss Ireland title.

For a very large sum of money at the time, Albert bought Harry Houdini's 'Substitution Trunk'. Billed by Houdini as the 'Metamorphosis' this was and still is the greatest magical illusion ever.

Metamorphosis – also known as 'The Substitution Trunk' was a spectacular illusion first performed by the legendary magician Harry Houdini and his wife Bessie in 1894. It was the trick that gained the Houdini's their first big tour with Welsh Brothers' circus in 1895. The trick is fast and amazing. The magician's hands would be fastened behind his back and he would be placed inside a large bag that was then padlocked. He was then placed inside a large trunk which was strapped closed and also padlocked. His assistant would stand on top of the trunk, raise a circular hoop of fabric over the trunk and count to three. On the third count the magician himself would drop the curtain and his assistant would be gone. When the trunk is opened his assistant is found inside the trunk inside the bag with the knots and seals unbroken and her hands secured in exactly the same way as her husband's. Wow! This was as slick an illusion as you could get and with unbelievable excitement, Albert and Betty began their practice. It would not be shown publicly until the following year.

In July 1958, they celebrated Louise's second birthday with visits to Rathgar to see the le Bas grandparents and then with tea in Donnybrook with Granny Merriman. It was a full-on day and Louise was spoilt shamelessly.

The absolute highlight of 1958 for Albert was of course the arrival of Dai Vernon in Ireland for the first time. For non-magical readers of this book, an explanation may be required here. Dai Vernon, also known as The Professor, was a Canadian magician whose expertise in sleight of hand techniques and his extensive knowledge of and dexterity with card tricks and close up magic, garnered him respect among fellow magicians the world over. His influence was considerable in the magic world of the twentieth century and he was a mentor to numerous famous magicians. He lived out his last years at the Magic Castle in Hollywood, California where he died in August 1992. His ashes are forever interred at the Magic Castle. But this was little old Ireland in 1958 and the 'God of Magic', probably the most revered magician in the world, was coming to Irish shores.

Albert had actually met Dai Vernon a few years earlier whilst on his honeymoon with Betty in London 1955. At this time, Dai had very generously cut a silhouette of their heads for the newlyweds. I have included the picture of these silhouettes at the start of this book not only because of the sheer skill of Dai Vernon to be able to just look at a person and cut their outline freehand, but because these cuttings were much treasured by Albert at the time and for many years later.

In 1958, the excitement among the magical community in Ireland was palpable. Even more special was that between lecturing to the Irish magicians in the Gresham Hotel and taking a quick trip to County Armagh where his grandfather hailed from, Dai Vernon came to spend the evening with Albert, Betty and some invited magicians in their home in Ballsbridge. Hubert and Kaye Lambert were there, as was Jack Sharp. A huge honour by any standards! Vernon did not disappoint and treated the assembled few to a very special performance of his famous 'Cups and Balls' routine.

He left Ireland to continue his lecture tour in England and remarked to a journalist of his time in the Emerald Isle: "I am very impressed by your Irish Magicians. Albert le Bas is as good as any I've seen." Praise indeed from the Maestro of Magic. In the coming years, Albert was to receive several letters from Dai by way of friendly chat, swapped stories of magic and best wishes. It was a relationship that Albert treasured.

Sometime later, on a normal everyday Tuesday, after washing and dressing little Louise, Betty was about to set out shopping and took a last check in the mirror before leaving the house. This was her usual practice, to look in the hall mirror, but this day was different. There might have been something in her eye, she may have been extra tired because the reflection that started back at her was double. Blinking and rubbing her eyes, she continued to stare but it did not make a difference, a small trickle of anxiety crept in. She looked around. In front of her were two Louise's, two hall doors and two hall tables. She sat down and waited. After about fifteen minutes all was well, her vision returned to normal and off she went. It must have been exhaustion, she dismissed it. It was hardly worth mentioning. But several weeks later something else odd happened. She was making curtains for the bathroom, nice blue and yellow chintz, using her trusty singer sewing machine, when for no particular reason her right foot seemed not to be able to hit the foot pedal. There was a strange pins and needles sensation in her whole leg which lasted a short while and then went away. She ignored it.

They were busy practicing every night with 'The Substitution'. They would launch this thrilling illusion to the audience for the first time on the Gaiety Theatre stage where they were special guest artists for the Jimmy O'Dea revue that year. 'The Substitution' performance was a roaring success and well worth the months of practice.

However, a few months later what Betty could no longer ignore was when the double vision returned and with it a seeming inability to get her right leg to move where she wanted it to. She stumbled in the kitchen and spilled a pot of tea. It lasted a couple of hours and passed. Betty thought it must surely be tiredness as they were celebrating the fantastic news that she was once again pregnant and expecting a second baby in the spring of 1959. They celebrated the news of the pregnancy and thankfully Betty did not appear to have any excessive signs of morning sickness so as they say in show business. The show must go on!

And on it did go with multiple appearances, accolades and write ups, with 'The Substitution' now the grand finale of most shows. On performance nights, her sister Nuala or her mother would arrive to dote over Louise. While Albert was changing into his custom-made dinner suits from Joe Monaghan or Siberry's of Dame Street, Dublin, Betty would pack her trusty round navy leather vanity case with Max Factor pan stick, luscious red lipstick, hair spray, fishnet stockings and a glitter costume with matching knickers. For a few hours, she would transport herself from being the suburban housewife into a world of glittering entertainment. By this time 'Albert le Bas and his beautiful wife' were quite the glamourous social couple on the Dublin entertainment scene but they still harboured longings of exposure and success in all corners of the world.

They set about making plans for this to happen. They scoured the international magic world for yet more daring and expensive illusions they could present to entertain and astound their audiences with. They were mindful to keep some evenings and days just for themselves. They had special date nights or romantic dinners to remind themselves yet again of their amazing good fortune, few financial worries, Albert's job, his magical success, the amazing support from their families and as always, their utter devotion to each other. Life could not possibly turn up any more roses.

Weekends were especially precious. Together, they took Louise to the park, tidied up the house and cared for their garden. The fruit trees bore luscious apples, pears and plums and each year they were picked and cleaned. The apples and pears were wrapped in newspaper and stored on cooling racks in the garage. Albert had planted a line of blackcurrant bushes at the end wall of the garden and Betty perfected the art of making delicious blackcurrant jam each year. Trips to the continent were planned to coincide with magical conventions. They flew with regularity to London, not just to shop for new tricks or illusions but at this time there were still items of clothing, household goods and sweets like Opal Fruits and Spangles, that were unavailable in Ireland and shops like Mothercare had different and very cute baby items. After all, Betty was nesting again.

What Betty thought about in the quiet lonely hours was the nagging feeling that something was not quite right. She was tired as any pregnant mother of a toddler would be tired, especially one who was also performing many nights a week. Perhaps even more tired than was expected. The odd bout of pins and needles had come back a few times fleetingly. Deep in the recesses of her mind was the unspoken fear that something major may be wrong.

Where had she heard of these random symptoms before? It was close to home. Well, she knew but was reluctant to entertain any such thoughts. Eddie her brother, her lovely gentle brother who was struggling with multiple sclerosis came to mind immediately. Had his illness not started a bit like this? Were his early symptoms similar? She tried in vain to empty her mind of these thoughts. The juggling of her various roles over the past few years had not been possible without the ever-present support of her Mum, who had become her confidante and trusted friend. For now, she needed to share her worries and deal with them before concerning Albert.

How could she tell her mother knowing the absolute heartache her dear mother was enduring with Eddie – all the doctors' appointments, the treatments that did not work, the great times when he seemed to be alright again and then the desperate times when he would relapse and his most basic physical functions would disappear overnight, the times he would suddenly be wracked with spasm and all around him were helpless to change anything for him, except wait for it to pass. No, how could she even begin to talk to her mum about what was happening for her. She could not suggest for one minute that she was having symptoms that she knew Eddie had experienced.

Her thoughts were drawn too to Mrs Brown, her mother's neighbour. Did her son not also have similar symptoms to Eddie and was now in long term care in a miserable nursing home? In fact, in later years she identified six young people in her childhood street that had similar symptoms. What if she was really sick and could no longer be a wife and mother? What would happen to Louise if she could not care for her? Oh my God, what about the new baby? She had to tell Albert of her concerns.

Tearfully, one evening when the house was quiet, dinner was over and their precious Louise tucked snugly into bed, she braved the conversation she was dreading. Albert listened and immediately cleared his schedule. Betty's health and the new pregnancy took absolute priority. Together, they visited the doctor. The local doctor on hearing the history of symptoms immediately referred Betty to a neurologist. After the neurologist appointment, Betty and Albert both came way silent and shocked.

The diagnosis was multiple sclerosis.

Effective treatment in 1958 was practically non-existent and the prognosis uncertain. She was a young, glamorous, active and pregnant mum with her whole life ahead of her. Betty was thirty years old.

Multiple sclerosis is a neurological condition where the protective coating of the nerves called myelin, is attacked by the body's own systems and eaten away. The result is that the brain is unable to send correct messages along the nerves to areas of the body to act as they should. In many cases, the picture of the disease is one of periods of attack and periods of remission. It can affect motor function and has been associated with emotional changes. There is no cure.

By the grace of God, as 1958 drew to a close, Betty's symptoms appeared to be in remission. She sailed along with her pregnancy, visiting her gynaecologist Dr Kevin Feeney, taking excellent care of Louise, and maintaining the home and of course, relishing her role on stage at every occasion.

The heart-breaking conversation with her mother had passed and with understanding and a true reflection of a mother's fierce love, Mary Merriman became her champion and support. There is a press photo of Betty at this time sitting atop The Substitution Trunk in a blue and silver shiny halter neck short costume, looking every bit the glamorous magician's assistant – the caption did not read that she was five months pregnant and living with multiple sclerosis.

Having toned things down a bit but still accepting a huge selection of engagements, Albert was spending more time at home with Betty. On April 7th, 1959, again in the Leinster Private Nursing Home, Albert and Betty welcomed into this world another perfect baby daughter whom they named Barbara Elizabeth Mary le Bas.

Now with two children to love and raise, Betty did not perform as much in the act. Albert continued with a full schedule and continued to work steadily, finding dinner dates and children shows in plentiful supply but of course as elsewhere, the variety theatre was dying. Alongside his paid performances, he kept up his steady habit of charity gigs. Concerts and parties arranged by religious orders, parish priests and charity organizations. It did not matter to him if you were dressed in mink or rags as each and every audience member mattered and was there to be entertained to the best of his ability.

Albert and Betty spent time with their non-magical friends, couples like Brian and Joan Hughes, Pete and Ellen Little. Like themselves, they were young parents navigating their way around this parenting thing. When they could, they would grab a night free from bottles and nappies, enjoy dinner or a play or just a few hours at the cinema.

Internationally, Ireland was perceived as a quaint isle populated by fairies and singing maidens. This image was cemented with the premier in Dublin of Walt Disney's film *Darby O'Gill and the Little People*. But the youth were listening to Radio Luxemburg and the first edition of the Irish Music Charts Top 10 was printed in the *Dublin Evening Herald*. Elvis Presley's *One Night* became the first song to top the charts. Things were very slowly changing. If anyone had asked what a teenager was, the reply would have been 'something new'.

That summer as well as staying as usual in Bettystown, Albert and Betty spent their summer holiday in Parknasilla, a hotel set on 500 acres overlooking Kenmare Bay on the Ring of Kerry. There were no shows, no audiences just a quiet little family having a break.

Later that same year, Albert was back on stage in the Gaiety Theatre in the role of 'Magicians Assistant' in the Jimmy O'Dea production of *Aladdin*. He shared the stage with the usual suspects, Vernon Hayden, Maureen Potter, Danny Cummins, Jimmy O'Dea and Milo O'Shea. It was a laugh out loud, roaring success.

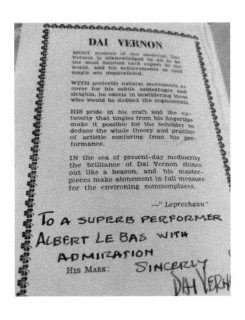

Barbara le Bas

Oofle Dust

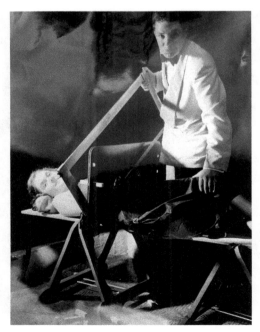

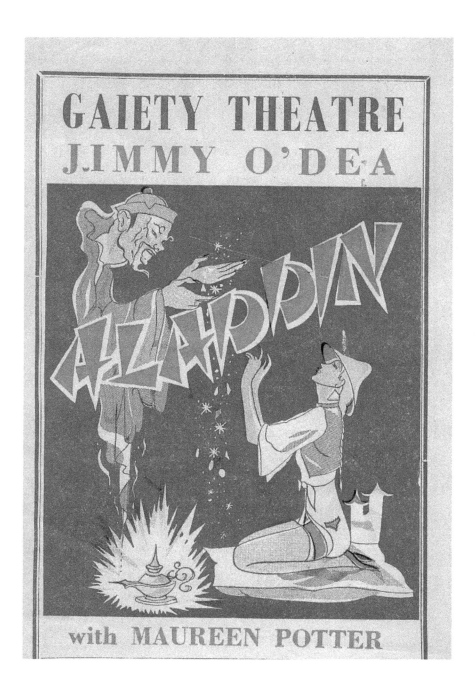

SCENE 4

—— ❧ ——

Arrived!

If our neighbours across the pond in England were swinging into the sixties, Ireland by comparison, was just learning how to sway. The Catholic Church maintained their vice-like grip on people's morality and even the term 'unisex' was deemed risqué. Outside of rural areas, in ever-growing towns and indeed in Dublin itself, suburban living was on the increase, partly due to the wider availability of a motor car as a result of a growing motor industry during the fifties, people now travelled a bit further from home to work or shop. The shopping centres arrived and Cornelscourt opened just south of Dublin.

In 1963, Ireland's first escalator was unveiled in Roches Stores on Henry Street. All very convenient for the women of Ireland who sadly still tightly held the role of second-class citizens. For the most part, they remained disallowed to work outside the home and whose roles were that of homemakers, wives and mothers. A quick glance at one of the questions on the Intermediate Certificate Examination Paper (Home Economics) in 1967 gives us a feel in what direction the education system was steering our young girls.

Marked 'For Girls Only' the question asks students:

Write detailed instructions of the care and cleaning of

(a) a kitchen sink,

(b) a waste bin,

(c) kitchen cutlery,

(d) glassware, and

(e) outdoor shoes.

Whilst Betty was indeed a mother and a housewife, she was certainly not a woman tied by the chattels of marriage into a life of domestic servitude. She was always quick to say that their marriage was a partnership on every level.

The arrival of UK television a few years earlier had opened the windows of the world to us, but it was still viewed by both the political and clerical hierarchy to potentially be as troublesome as communism. As a safeguard, television sets were few and far between. Albert and Betty were lucky to have one. Later, they described the reception, all in black and white to be like watching a programme through a snowstorm.

This duo faced a new decade with youth and gusto, a decade that would bring with it many new experiences and thrills. This was the boom time.

In 1960, Albert was President of the SIM and during the ensuing year, he made a presentation to secretary Neta Kelly at the North-South get-together. At the annual dinner, a presentation was also made to Goodliffe. Harold Taylor attended a meeting as he was in town appearing at the Theatre Royal with Jimmy Shand & his Band. Albert was engaged for special appearances at the summer shows at Butlins Holiday camp in Mosney, and once again took to the road for the long drive to the show and returned home each night. Starting on July 25th that year, he performed in the Gaiety Theatre Summer Show Flights of Fancy with again Jimmy O'Dea, Edmund Brown, Vernon Hayden and Danny Cummins.

I cannot find any records of trips to the UK, but I am sure that there were – more conventions, more new gags and tricks and lots of awe and bafflement as other magicians showed off their acts.

Later that year in October 1960, Albert was engaged to perform at a house party for the Viscountess De Vesci at their home in Abbeyleix. This was a trip he had made before that must have been a success because he was asked back.

The following year, Albert was again elected President of the SIM and never failed to attend a meeting. The society was growing, and it was an exciting time to be a young hopeful magician in Ireland.

On the home front, another exciting event happened in 1961. Louise, now five years old, was off to school. Despite frowning on the part of Albert's mother who felt that children were only properly educated under the tutelage of either the Loretto nuns or the Jesuit priests, Louise was enrolled in the Dominican Convent Muckross Park school in Donnybrook and started her kindergarten days all togged out in her pale green smock. It took a few weeks for her to settle and Albert delivered her every morning just before the bell and waved her into the classroom. He was standing in the same spot every day without fail, waiting to collect her when school time was over. For a long time, Louise believed that he just waited patiently outside the door all morning. Sometime during that first term in 1961, school photos were taken and Louise with her dark hair in a clip and her piercing dark eyes was lined up with a few of her fellow classmates, looking very serious and holding a Veritas reader. It was a photo that the nuns had it framed and mounted on the corridor wall. Many years later in 1986, I had occasion to visit Muckross Park in my capacity as a judge for the Interschools Mental Health Debating Competition and there on the way into the school concert hall hung the picture with Louise's little face staring back at me.

1961 arrived and on Saturday January 7th, 1961, Albert was invited down to Abbeyleix to the home of the Viscountess De Vesci. A venue not unknown to him as he had entertained there twice before for private parties. Newly married HRH Princess Margaret and her husband Anthony Armstrong Jones, later to become Lord Snowden, were visiting and some superb entertainment was required of Albert. Fourteen guests, so said the *Dublin Evening Mail*, enjoyed the forty-five-minute performance. Albert told Chris Woodward afterwards that although a little nervous, he had been reassured by the head footman, who, in Albert's words 'marked my card' as to the correct protocol and etiquette for such an occasion.

It is not known what Albert's programme was on that auspicious evening, but one can be assured he wouldn't have tried anything new, so maybe the Misers Dream and The Giant Rising Cards were part of his programme. The thought of him asking HRH to please say 'Arise your Majesty' for the Queen of Hearts to rise would not have been removed from the script! Unlike today, security would not have been an issue then as it was a simple low-key family visit. The performance, more than likely in intimate surroundings, would have been a memorable, well-earned and well-deserved accolade not only for Albert but his family too. Knowing him as a true pro, he would have taken it all in his stride. There is a letter amongst Alberts things to an unknown person in which he further describes this visit, he states 'I had a good chat with Mr Armstrong Jones, and he is a lovely chap.'

As an aside, Chris Woodward also had the honour of appearing before HRH Princess Margaret, a few years later. But this time Albert beat him to it!

In contrast to a royal audience, just a week later Albert along with Jack Cruise, Paddy Crosby, Joe Lynch, Edmund Brown and many others gave an equally professional performance at the annual concert for the inmates of Mountjoy Prison in Dublin.

Another summer season at Red Island in Skerries followed, and so too did the time for another family holiday with just Betty and the girls. During Albert's presidential year at the SIM, there was a special dinner on October 4th, 1961. At the dinner, a presentation was made by Albert to Tommy Cooper who was visiting Ireland on holiday. Later in the year during the week of October 23rd, a visit was made by a group from the Society to The Mahatma Circle in Liverpool, and a similar presentation once again of an inscribed Shillelagh was made by Albert to US top magician, historian, author and illusionist Milbourne

Christopher who was appearing that week at the Liverpool Empire in 'Christopher's Wonders'.

Albert presided over and, of course, did a spot at the SIM Annual Convention that was held in Howth that year. Then, finally, along came television and with it, a myriad of opportunities for Albert in his home country. In December 1961, the soon-to-be launched Irish television station *Telefís Eireann* announced its plans for light entertainment. Outlining what was needed as "a mixture of entertainment which will not debase public standards and matters of cultural and educational content which will not tend to make viewers switch off their sets or turn to a different channel."

A considerable portion of the stations programmes was to be made up of light entertainment, light music, variety shows, Westerns, detective stories and adventure films. The controller of programmes, Mr Michael Barry, was reported to have deliberately sought out matters of the highest entertainment standard. Opening night was to see Maureen Potter, Jimmy O'Dea and Mary O'Hara in *Céad Míle Fáilte* (A hundred Thousand Welcomes). Of course, Albert was on the show too!

The contracts from *Telefís Eireann* began rolling in and Albert landed a plum job being compère of Irish television's top weekend show, *Curtain Up*. This was the equivalent of the UK show *Sunday Night at the London Palladium*. He signed a thirteen-week contract for the princely sum of twenty-five pounds a performance.

In May that year, Albert featured in a large pictorial in the *Sunday Independent* newspaper. He was preparing for the annual SIM convention in the Ormond Hotel in Dublin. As a publicity stunt, he gave veiled hints to hotel management that there was every possibility the hotel itself may actually vanish during the convention due to the intensity of strange vibes and spells that would be flying around, as can happen when a collection of magicians wield their wands in unison. Just in case, he took out an insurance police with Lloyds Insurers in London. Thankfully, the hotel remained intact!

Between filming with RTE, his day job, being father to two delightful girls and attentive husband to Betty, Albert also completed the 1962 summer season at Mosney and attended the Brighton British Ring Convention. There his performance was again lauded in *Gen* magazine by Harry Stanley who wrote: "Albert Le Bas of Ireland was in great form with Misers Dream and Balloon Modelling. (With small assistance from the audience) Albert is a grand entertainer." The *Abra* write up was equally as positive: "Albert Le Bas followed – good, sound commercial stuff – Misers Dream amongst the audience and balloon modelling. That doesn't do him justice; he was on top form. I never saw him better and feel sure he never will be and doesn't need to."

Closer to home, Albert was wielding a different kind of magic! To their delight, Betty and Albert celebrated the news of yet a third pregnancy with the new baby due in mid-1963. They could not have been happier. Betty's health was holding, the MS was slowly manifesting itself and she walked now with a limp and was easily tired. Ever practical, they hired a cleaning lady to help with the household chores. Betty still buzzed around Dublin in her Hillman Imp and chased after her two growing daughters, visited her mother and delighted in her sister Nuala's new relationship.

She never let her creative side fade and she took to sewing with a passion, ensuring that the girls always had matching or complimentary outfits for every occasion. I was told years later – how true it is I have no idea – that there were certain parishioners from the Queen of Peace Church who only went to ten o'clock mass on a Sunday to see what new and outrageous outfits the le Bas girls were wearing!

Even without stage appearances, magic consumed a lot of her time, she was hostess to multiple visiting magicians, attended social soirees with Bertie, and spent hours on the preparation that went into ensuring that Albert's tricks were fault free. As was their custom by now, she was a critical and attentive audience of one while Albert practiced and practiced his act.

Nestling within the Wicklow mountains with its unique waterfall, the highest in Ireland, is Powerscourt House. An imposing Palladian style stately home once owned by Lord Powerscourt (of the Wingfield Verner family) and it is now currently owned by the Slazenger family. There are two ironic coincidences with magic and Powerscourt.

The first is that Dai Vernon the Canadian born magician whose real name is David Wingfield Verner is distantly related to the earlier owners, the Wingfield Verner family. Secondly, when the son of the new owner Michael Slazenger celebrated his 21st birthday in 1962, it was a truly lavish affair with guests arriving in horse-drawn carriages or in some cases, even on horseback. The famous UK society bandleader, Tommy Kinsman, was engaged to play for the guests during the five-hour extravaganza. The cabaret was comedian Milo O'Shea and Albert le Bas with his magic. It was one of the highlights of the Irish social calendar that year.

Many years later, tragedy was to strike the Slazenger family and Michael sadly died when his light aircraft crashed on landing on the private airstrip within the grounds of the estate.

August and September 1962 saw Albert again treading the boards of the Gaiety Theatre in the Actors Equity Production 'Pick of the Pops'. This was a riotous show with dancers, comedy, magic – of course, and singing, all the ingredients that he loved. And so too apparently did the faithful Dublin theatregoers.

Yvonne Josephine Mary le Bas entered the world on June 9th, 1963 at Mount Carmel Private Hospital – another gorgeous daughter for Albert and Betty and finally their family was complete. With Yvonne's arrival also came the notion to extend the family home. Plans were drawn up and a large extension at the back of the house took shape comprising of a new square kitchen and above it a fourth bedroom, like the other three – complete with personal washbasin. Betty was in her element, juggling children and interior design, she somehow managed to not only paint the whole place but to also make all the soft furnishings for the bedroom, in shades of pale green and mauve.

Louise and I shared the room with single beds covered in matching raspberry coloured candlewick spreads, a big picture window overlooking the Merrion Riding School and an unused but very decorative cast iron fireplace at one end. The box room was now transformed into a magical storeroom where Albert's tricks and smaller illusions were stored and meticulously labelled. As a completely irrelevant fact, one of the carpenters working on the extension apparently also moonlighted as an encyclopaedia salesman. This was how we acquired a complete set of encyclopaedias and a set of blue leather-bound classics that I still have today.

The RTE Variety Show continued each season in the early sixties with Albert as its host, but by 1964 it had been replaced by an ever-increasing parade of foreign TV material. Albert still performed on Irish TV and during 1964 and 1965, appeared weekly on the light entertainment show *Coisir Samhraidh* – a show that was rehearsed in Studio 3 in Montrose between 3.45pm and 4.15pm, and then went to air live for forty-five minutes.

On May 24th, 1963, Albert began what was to become a most fulfilling and rewarding relationship that would last for many years and for which he is perhaps most remembered.

Jurys Hotel on Dame Street, Dublin opened its doors to a new era in entertainment – a dinner and cabaret catering to tourists. Several factors collided to make this cabaret a roaring success. In the sixties, it became part of a new outward-looking Ireland that was moving to compete with other European nations for the tourist dollar. For many years, the children of thousands of Irish emigrants to the United States of America had filled their children and their children's heads with stories of the 'Old sod', a mystical emerald isle where dark haired maidens danced at the crossroad, old men sang and played pipes and whistles, where whole communities gathered at the drop of a hat to talk, tell stories and drink a very dark beer. A dream that was perpetuated by the 1952 film *The Quiet Man* starring John Wayne and fuelled Americans expectations of Irish culture before they could even step off the Aer Lingus onto the tarmac. The Irish were savvy to the stereotypes and embraced them for commercial reasons. They gave the tourists what they were expecting because they wanted them to come back.

Ireland was ready, and Jurys cabaret delivered the nostalgic dream and then some. If the tourists wanted to hear Galway Bay or Danny Boy, that's what was served up. Literally 'served up' as the opening act in the early days was a hearty welcome from the singing Chef – Vernon Hayden. Irish dancers? No problem. The girls and boys from the Rory O'Connor School of Dancing danced their little hearts out, the pretty young Dublin singers in quaint costumes looking like extras from *The Quiet Man* sang the ballads and tunes the visitors had come to hear and the big numbers – the sad songs of loss, longing and emigration, of families separated, of nationalist pride and determination. They were delivered at a rousing pace by talented tenors and baritones. All in a terrific recipe for success. The show was produced by Fred O'Donovan the managing director and producer-in-chief of Eamonn Andrews Studios Ltd., who had been involved with over 300 radio shows every year, numerous commercial films and many live shows.

Albert was an integral part of the inaugural and subsequent shows for many years. He emceed the whole thing, artfully meshing the acts with gags and quick tricks and then of course performing his own 'spot'. He started with Jurys in 1963. For five months every year until 1968, he worked the crowds in Jurys seven nights a week from May to November. Along the way, the cabaret moved from its original home in Dame Street to the site of the former Intercontinental Hotel in Ballsbridge. Many talented artists shared the boards with him including singers Edmund Brown, John McNally, Mary Sheridan and Claire Kelleher, ventriloquist and puppeteer Eugene Lambert, the fiddle playing Carroll family complete with Aran sweaters and at a later stage, the company was joined by comedian Hal Roach and singer Tony Kenny. Apart from write ups in the Irish papers, the following year a review from a magical perspective, again in *Abra*, appeared about his Jurys performance.

"What you don't know is how hard he works in the show. I went along to find out last Wednesday evening.

The entertainment is in a large ballroom on a dais – one could fairly call it a stage except in the sense that the term is used in a nightclub. It's a platform without footlights, curtains or orchestra pit. It does have a revolving 'stage' to overcome some of the disabilities and it's maybe amusing to know that at the final dress rehearsal when the revolve signal was given, a man pressed the button and the electric motor blew up so for the first six weeks of the run two chaps had to push the thing round by hand. The audience sits at tables. For the most part, they are American and other overseas visitors. Capacity is about 250 and on quieter nights attendance is around 150. Albert, the compère, starts the thing off by entering 'cold' – not even a musical chord, steps up to the mike and welcomes the visitors. He explains that the show is '*Siamsa Mór*' which is Irish for a big party. He mixes with the people finding out where they come from invites them to enjoy themselves and introduces the first act. A trio of Irish harpists who are discovered 'on' as the stage revolves.

There are Irish dancers also on the bill. They got a very good hand. One of them is a child of eight and you can't compete with child artists. Irish vocalists, an Irish girl piper and drummer who made a terrific entrance in the spotlight.... and Albert. It's fair to say – and I've given this a lot of thought because I'm prejudiced in favour of magicians that, save for a couple of odd moments, the show came alive each time Albert appeared and was otherwise humdrum.

Albert appeared about eight times. He did, in total, his standard act and more besides. I noted the Egg Bag (with a small glass of whisky), his Misers Dream using a child's seaside bucket with which he dashed through the auditorium extracting coins most convincingly from the hair and clothing of spectators – It's about the best version of this effect I've seen! – working at breakneck speed. Giant Rising Cards and Mutilated Sunshade worked with a girl volunteer from the audience, who is rewarded with a balloon animal and as I probably said before, Albert packs into the making of this one figure just about all that is worth using in the balloon modelling field.

Pause for breath and onto Troublewit, which he works fast along the lines of Claude Perry, The Himber Linking Finger Rings (he uses the original Himber article) – two borrowed rings apparently linked and examined and unlinked right down amongst the spectators, and Cards From Pocket which degenerates into a production of any card you like asked for. An insurance card, a birthday card, a valentine card, and so on. I wish I didn't have to keep saying 'worked very fast' but I must, because it is true and indeed, I don't know of anyone who works faster or more consistently. Interspersed with some gags like the Chicken Sandwich – Spring Chicken between two huge slices of bread.

All really hard work, really good clean magic allied with polish and charm for one show it would be a great achievement. As a non-stop stampede of perhaps 150 performers, it strikes me as well-nigh unbeatable and make no mistake, Albert doesn't just hold the show together, he virtually IS the show."

I visited the show hundreds of times. I remember the early days in Dame Street because you would be seated up on the balcony. Later in Ballsbridge, you could stand backstage, just at the stage side in readiness for the Irish Dancers to turn and high kick inches from your face. Beautiful harp music was provided by the Sion Hill Harpists and when I attended Sion Hill School myself as a student, I think Albert harboured hopes that I too would learn the harp and become one of the singers. One short singing audition with the singing coach however, soon squashed that dream as I could not then nor now hold a note! I loved the songs, knew all the words but woe and betide anyone within earshot if I ever sing! As we got older, I think we all enjoyed the night for different reasons – the thrill of anticipation when Dad came on, the pleasure of the rousing applause and when I was about twelve, the desperate hope that Noel Carroll would wink at you!

I do not think that Albert's absence from home life seven nights a week for five months each year was a source of distress, mostly because we could go with him 'to the show' any night. Though, I am assuming not on a school night! The second thing that softened the blow was that he often came home with dinner that the chef had cooked for himself and Betty and if you were still awake, you could position yourself on the top of the stairs when he came through the door and would invariably be included in the midnight dinner with your parents.

My older sister, Louise, tells me that at the end of the season all the artists received a bonus. Albert and Betty would buy us children a special present at that time. Alas, I don't have any recollection of this. On this night, the Jurys chef would prepare an extra special meal for us all and we ate it late at night in our dining room which Betty would have prepared with white linen table cloths, the 'good' Waterford crystal and Wedgewood china and candles to mark the end of yet another successful season.

What I do know is that here yet again, was another source of new friends that over the years became figures in our young lives. We knew the Lambert children from the Jurys days but after we moved to Monkstown, Eugene and May Lambert and their ten children also moved to this suburb, so we saw a lot of them. They went on to open Ireland's first Puppet Theatre in a mews at the rear of their large home in Clifton Terrace, Monkstown. Austin Gaffney and his wife Agnes were frequent visitors at home. John McNally became an amazing support to Albert and, of course, Fred and Sally O'Donovan were part of the clan.

Although Albert remained booked for seven nights a week for five months of the year for the next few years, it did not prevent him from accepting other engagements and he never neglected his charity causes. As always, he returned home every single night to Betty and the girls, no matter where in Ireland he was performing. He was never an absent father and again in 1964, when I followed Louise to Muckross Park School, it was Albert who took us there every day.

Magically speaking, the biggest highlight perhaps of 1964 was in March of that year. The Diamond Jubilee of the British Magical Society took place in the Midland Institute in the centre of Birmingham, and both Albert and Chris Woodward appeared on the same show. The report in the BMS monthly magazine stated that 'a slick and professional Albert Le Bas presented a superb Misers Dream, Rising Cards, and closed with wonderful balloon modelling'. Goodliffe confirmed with his own report that Albert 'was tremendous with his professional and polished act, and faultless magic which packed enormous fun into the items already described. He only makes one animal but in so doing, he brings in all the worthwhile balloon stunts'.

In April of the same year, the SIM Silver Jubilee Convention was held at the Royal Hotel in Bray and Albert again appeared.

Chris Woodward writes…

In the month of August, the legendary card worker Dai Vernon had travelled over from New York on the Queen Mary with his long-time friend Jay Ose from the Magic Castle. My parents drove down to Cobh in Southern Ireland to pick them up and on their journey up to Dublin they enjoyed the green scenery. One vivid memory was Jay telling Dai. 'Look Dai… cows and sheep!' Something not readily seen in the city of their home city of Los Angeles! I was flattered when they said that they would be happy to stay with us in Killiney, County Dublin and in doing so, we all spent a happy time reminiscing about magic and magicians. I vividly recall Albert and family visiting us and him presenting his own version of the Cups and Balls to Dai and Jay who were both highly impressed with his presentation. During this visit, Dai cut my silhouette that I later used it as an image for my bookplate. We took them both to Powerscourt to see where Dai's ancestor lived. This picture shows Jay offering his wallet to Dai with insufficient funds to buy the house!

The Magic Castle in Hollywood is a truly unique magical location and the highly revered Dai lived there for many of his later years and reached the wonderful age of ninety-eight before he passed away. Jay was the first resident magician at The Castle in 1963 but being a heavy smoker sadly died aged only fifty-five. Individually, they were hugely talented within magic circles and also great characters, the likes of which don't seem to be around anymore.

On August 23rd that year at Jurys Hotel, Dai Vernon and Jay Ose were hosted by the Society of Irish Magicians. In a programme arranged by long-time correspondent and friend, Hubert Lambert, Dai Vernon gave a lecture at 3.30pm. This was followed by Dinner at 6.00pm then at 7.00pm Jay Ose, The Resident Magician at The Magic Castle Hollywood, gave his wonderful offering. After their short stay in Dublin they both flew to London where they gave several lectures for Harry Stanley before flying on to Hamburg.

Albert was an avid writer to both family, friends, fans and magical colleagues. How he would have loved today's technology of video calls, webinars and instant text messages. But the media of the day was letter writing and he faithfully kept in touch with all.

In the Baghdad column of *Gen Magazine*, it was mentioned how grateful the Larsen family were for the gift of shamrock on St Patrick's Day. Once again, this highlights Albert's thoughtfulness and kindness.

1965 saw Sam Mercer present Albert with the 'Magician of the Year Trophy' that had two years previously been donated by USA magicians Tom Hawbecker, Dick du Bois and Ace Gorham who had visited Ireland, Dublin in particular. It meant so much to both himself and Betty that he was recognised amongst the purveyors of his own craft.

Goodliffe had flown to America in the 50s with a small group of other magicians, namely his sidekick Tom Harris – The Magical Schoolmaster, the FISM winner Geoffrey Buckingham, Max Andrews the magical dealer from London and manipulator John Ramsay from Scotland. It was following that successful visit that Goodliffe founded The Flying Sorcerers.

One had to be invited to join but the qualifications were such that you had to fly to The United States to appear at one of their magic conventions. In later years, many flew over, some even travelled by boat and were desperate to join, but as I say, they did not qualify unless they were actually invited. It was rather exclusive to be a member. At the beginning of 1965 in *Abra*, and in trying to promote the IBM convention Goodliffe said, "Let's make our slogan for 1965, 'The Flying Sorcerers Fly Again!'" Well, they certainly did and with little encouragement too!

Here was a golden opportunity for Albert to nibble away at his ultimate dream of performing in all corners of the world – America. But plans had to be made, it was a trip of more than two weeks and himself and Betty had three children to consider. There was no way he would have travelled without Betty. Still holding her own and looking beautiful, her only visible disability was perhaps a leg that dragged a bit and a right side that would not have been nimble enough to manipulate any props, but boy, was she excited! They turned again to Granny Merriman to save the day and arrangements were made for the three girls to stay with her in Donnybrook for the duration of the trip. This worked out well as both Louise and Barbara were in school in Marlborough Road, Donnybrook, and it was only a short walk from Granny Merriman's house.

Meanwhile, Albert's mother who was a whiz at crochet, was on task to produce several beautiful crocheted tops for Betty for the trip, including the most gorgeous short sleeved evening top in dark green with midnight blue flashed through with a sparkling thread of shimmering aqua – a perfect match for a short velvet skirt that Betty had made to match. Despite the MS, her legs were still shapely, and she could carry off the 1960s shorter style skirt with the best of them! Red TWA carry-on bags appeared in our home, passports, travel plans and sunblock filled the kitchen counters.

In June 1965, they were off!

Chris writes: "Along with Albert and others, I was fortunate to be invited to attend the International Brotherhood of Magicians Convention in Des Moines Iowa. In fact, Albert was absolutely thrilled. It had been a long-time ambition to appear in America and at last, his dream had come true. The grand top of the bill attraction was none other than Joseph Dunninger, the famous Magician and Mentalist and a big friend and confidante of Harry Houdini. He had never attended a magician's convention before, so it was a real coup to get him on the gala show.

Due to work commitments at Jurys, Albert and Betty had made their own travel arrangements. They had been met at New York's JFK Airport by none other than old friend Mystic Craig and British Ring stalwart Bill Stickland. It was reported how much Albert & Betty were thrilled to be met by familiar faces. Craig, as he was affectionately known, gave them welcome hospitality and kindly saw to their travel needs returning them to the airport and then they flew on to Des Moines airport, arriving well before the group that Goodliffe had assembled. The main party had flown into Chicago from London Heathrow with a very brief turnaround that enabled a few of us to travel into town to Jay Marshall's shop. We asked the taxi to wait whilst we popped in to say a 'quick ten-minute hello' to Jay and Dai Vernon and then promptly whizzed back to the airport for our onward journey.

Within a very short time of arriving at the Des Moines hotel, Tom Harris, Chris Woodward, Albert and Goodliffe had been whisked away to the local TV station where they promoted the convention and the gala show with each doing some small magic before the TV cameras.

The convention was well organised and for every person registered, there was even a convention badge that had a magical puzzle theme.

One of the main attractions of any magic convention is not only the brotherhood and conviviality with meeting old and making new friends, but also the magical dealers. This is usually housed in a guarded room all to themselves, where individual magic suppliers offer their new and old items for sale. Albert, having experienced his own emporium with The Druids Den, was in his element searching out the apparatus that would suit him best. It is not known if he actually acquired anything but the thrill of just looking at what was new or old was great, nevertheless. It is said that if the dealers do well, the convention is considered a great success. For them at least!

The other wonderful thing about this type of national/international convention is actually meeting names, both famous and infamous, that you had read about over the years and in doing so, you build up a rapport with them for future meetings or at least, correspondence in between – snail mail back then naturally, as the internet hadn't been invented.

The convention as a whole was a great success, and Albert scored well, in fact very well, indeed. Albert appeared in the close-up segment with his Himber Rings presentation, he compèred another show and also appeared on the grand gala too in the 1,200 seat Paramount Theatre. All the way through, he wisely used material that was tried and tested and honed to perfection over the many appearances he had made at Jurys.

After the first gala show performance we, that is Albert and I, were both 'talent spotted' by Mark Leddy the highly respected and experienced 'talent scout' for the Ed Sullivan Television Show that was just about to go into colour. Due to travel problems the producer of the show who had the final say fell ill with a severe case of food poisoning and couldn't make our second show at Fantasy Land in Buffalo and so for both of us – whether black and white or colour, the much sought after TV appearance never happened! However, it was flattering to be able to say we qualified by someone as experienced as Mr Leddy!

Goodliffe had known Gene Gordon for many years as Gene was one of the three original founding members of the International Brotherhood of Magicians. After an appearance in Fantasy Land Buffalo, and a quick visit to Niagara Falls, the next stop for the whole magic party was to visit Chicago.

Magic Inc. was the magic shop to end all shops with lovable Frances & Jay Marshall in charge. In the back of the shop there was a small intimate theatre where Albert also entertained, charming the audience yet again with his magical masterpiece 'Misers Dream'. It was a strange coincidence that Fran Marshall's first husband was Laurie Ireland.

A quick flight to Milwaukee and another magic convention. This time The Society of American Magicians were holding their annual gathering. Goodliffe again reported that all the acts acquitted themselves more than admirably and one of his favourite editorial expressions was he 'rattled through' his well-known act. Albert was a virtual whirlwind – no better praise indeed.

It was said by another travelling companion that their stay was cut short due to Betty being homesick. Having left three delightful daughters behind aged just ten, five and just two years of age, it was no wonder!"

To think that Betty spent this time away from her children feeling sad or guilty is perhaps a slight misnomer. She shopped! Oh boy, did she shop! I have no idea of travel luggage allowances back in the 1960s but Betty came home with multiple sets of towels from Marshall and Field, a ridiculous amount of American clothes for her daughters, several handbags and hats and best of all for Louise and myself – Barbie Dolls. These were relatively new toys on the American market having been launched just a few years previously and had not yet reached Irish, nor indeed UK shores.

Louise got an original Barbie complete with a medically impossible body and long blond locks, and I being younger, got a doll of the Barbie family 'Tammy', her slightly more underdeveloped cousin. Along with the dolls, their own dressing tables and wardrobes for each of us, Albert and Betty had splurged on several packages of Barbie clothing, all I think were variations of Jackie Onassis outfits, right down to accessories, including miniature strings of pearls. We played with those dolls for years. And Betty fuelled our passion by sourcing Vogue patterns for new Barbie outfits and spending countless hours sewing miniscule hooks and eyes onto outfits. Can you believe it – Vogue patterns for new Barbie outfits! I still have a naked, by now fifty-year-old, Tammy in a box in my attic. Oh, how I wish someone had told me not to bite off the fingernails of Louise's original doll because I do believe that they are worth a considerable fortune today.

Of this trip to America Chris writes: "Thanks to Goodliffe's wonderful connections in Chicago one of the highlights of the '65 US trip was a visit to the home of Gene Bernstein. He was very well known obviously in magic circles but at that time he was unknown to me. The Goodliffe party was requested to Gene's penthouse apartment high up overlooking Chicago. We were feted like never before. The hospitality of the Americans is well known but this was something else. There was food and drinks galore. Lots of local 'names' were present, and we all reciprocated by doing a little magic for everyone. Although small in number, Goodlife's party that naturally included Albert and Betty, was maybe a dozen at the most. Gene said, "Come, get into my car and I will show you Chicago."

I couldn't figure out how he was going to fit us all in, but a massive car awaited us downstairs by the lobby. He drove us all around the main areas of downtown Chicago. Apart from the size of the car, the one thing that I remember most was the highway barriers that, depending on the rush hour time of day, they rose and fell into the road-way making four lanes going into the centre in the morning, with two lanes coming out, but at night time the barriers would change and the four lane highway was for the massive work traffic that would leave the city in the evening. It was all hydraulically controlled of course but a wonderful idea to keep the volume of traffic moving.

The following day friends asked did we get to ride in Gene's car. Yes, was the prompt reply, but guess what was so special about the car? It was bulletproof! That in itself was fascinating but to find out why added the cherry on the cake. It seems that Gene, a highly successful lawyer, had at one time defended Al Capone. Not only that but had got him off the charge! Whether this was just a story or the truth, it didn't really matter. It made the visit to Gene's apartment and his generous hospitality one that none of us would ever forget."

Upon the return home, Albert was both thrilled and excited to learn that he too had been accepted into Goodliffe's exclusive Flying Sorcerers Society! It was a rare and unique organisation in that it had NO subscriptions, NO rules and NO meetings!

After they came home in July, Goodliffe reported in *Abra* #1015 that he visited Dublin again on business and complimented Albert that he had been chosen to appear on the Magic Circle Scala Show. As the last time the show had been put on was nine years ago, he mischievously added, "a quick return visit by popular demand!" He also took time to visit Albert where he was still appearing seven times a week at Jurys Hotel. So successful was the show with the tourists, that a fortnight's extension was proposed. Goodliffe went on in his article setting out that by his reckoning, Albert would have made 168 consecutive performances multiplied by six years, which became a formidable total!

Also that year in September while Albert was in the middle of a thirteen-week TV series for children, he flew to London for the day on Wednesday July 7th, recording a television appearance on the Rolf Harris 'Hey Presto It's Rolf' series for the BBC and was back home again that night for his appearance at Jurys! In the limited timeslot available, the two items he used were the Himber Rings and a Cup and Ball. The show was also shown abroad in Africa and I still have the never-banked cheque framed for the repeat performance in the princely sum of three shillings!

Later that year, Albert was engaged by The Magic Circle to entertain on their annual festive show at the Scala Theatre in London's West End. The programme was televised by the BBC and was broadcast on November 11th, 1965. Due to the prestigious honour of this appearance, it was also written up in the Irish newspapers. Sadly, as it was a live show there is no actual recording of the TV programme in the BBC archive.

The magical journals report of the stage show was as follows:

Albert le Bas — Ireland's Leading Magician — was given a warm welcome and his presentation of the Miser's Dream using a child's seaside bucket to catch the coins he produced from thin air was an instant success with the audience. Using two packs of cards, one regular size and one jumbo size, Albert presented an excellent rising card effect – the cards selected by members of the audience from the small pack being duplicated by the cards which subsequently rose from the large-size pack. This large-size pack rested in a giant liqueur glass which stood on a table well away from the performer and seemingly quite unaided, obeyed commands and caused the cards to rise as directed. A surprise finish to this effect was the rising of the four of spades (wrong card) and the instantaneous and visible change by sliding two of the pips to make the six of spades (correct card). With the help of a young assistant from the audience who just could not blow out Albert's re-light taper, the Human Gasometer, with the long glass tube and a gas mantle was performed. Finally, a great deal of fun was extracted from blowing up balloons to make a model giraffe with its long neck and legs. Thanking his young assistant and rewarding him with the giraffe, Albert made his exit to the loud applause he so rightly deserved.

The following year. Goodlife was in Dublin again on business and naturally met up with Albert as he had always done when time permitted. At that time in O'Connell Street, the pillar and statue to Lord Nelson stood proud as it had done since 1808. Goodliffe and Albert had lunch. The following night and although no connection with their meeting, a loud explosion occurred – Irish dissidents had blown up the statue and pillar. It was said the following night two heads of Nelson were offered for sale in different parts of London. Though how true this joke is, I cannot say!

Albert was in his third annual consecutive season at Jurys Hotel, and had the added bonus of an appearance by Eugene Lambert, the well-known local puppeteer and ventriloquist. Once again, it was a seven-night contract for a six-month season that was to be followed by a month's tour of the USA. The USA tour did not actually happen for Albert, despite the longing. Betty was slowly becoming more unwell and with three young children to care for, Albert passed on a second trip to the states and instead, carried on with his Irish appearances.

Albert was exhausted, and in the middle of the Jurys season that year, he was hospitalised for pleurisy and pneumonia. After a short recovery period, he resumed his role in Jurys on Monday August 15th. In his absence, his place been taken by Count de Reski, aka Tony Thursby.

The year finished with the usual Christmas parties and engagements for his faithful customers and a welcome break at home with no dates. He did appear on the RTE pre-recorded Christmas Crackers Show which was aired on Christmas Day. For this festive show he performed the Dolls House Illusion, producing both Louise and myself from the empty box with me being slightly peeved. This I distinctly remember, because despite my beautiful pink satin floor length costume, I was not wearing the dress I coveted – Louise's blue spotted 'shower of hail' dress with a row of pink velvet ribbons down the front! At six years old, I was obviously quite the diva!

Albert's other act on that show was the sawing in half, not using his slim assistant Betty this time, instead it was Irish actor and sometimes comedian, Milo O'Shea.

1966 brought a rather strange request of Albert. He was contacted by a producer called Harry Alan Towers of the USA film company, American International Pictures. They were planning a new film starring Vincent Price, Martha Hyer and George Nades called '*House of 1,000 Dolls*'. It was the story of holidaymakers in Tangiers who stumble across an establishment where an illusionist captures unsuspecting victims for the white slave trade. The film was to be made in Ardmore Studios in Bray, County Wicklow. Vincent Price, in the lead role of a nightclub magician, needed to be taught some magic tricks and Albert was to be his tutor.

Given the script, Albert set about making some stage illusions befitting a dodgy nightclub. One item in particular, a huge golden cone on a stand (what its purpose was, I have no idea) remained in our garden shed for years. Eventually the film was not shot in Ardmore Studios but in Madrid, Spain. Albert's services were not required and when the film was released in the USA, it got terrible reviews and was noted to have been 'quite possibly the sleaziest movie AIP ever made'.

By now it is 1967, baby Yvonne is four and their other daughters are growing up so fast. Things are changing in Ireland. Jacqueline Kennedy arrived in Ireland for a holiday and immediately the shops were filled with look-alike fashion items. Eamon De Valera held strong as the Irish President and Jack Lynch of the Fianna Fáil party was Taoiseach (Prime Minister). Later that same year, the Minister for Education Donogh O'Malley made a surprise announcement of free secondary school education for all from 1969.

The young people in Ireland had truly embraced the concept of teenagers and were walking far away from their parents parochial and innocent values. They were listening to Pink Floyd who performed their only ever Irish concert in Cork's Arcadia Ballroom in September of that year. Strangely, in this year there was also a big revival in Irish music and song – a backlash perhaps to the selling out of our traditions to attract the tourists and make us a nation more homogeneous with other European destinations. There was a new celebration of the Irish language and Celtic values, not driven this time, by clerical decree or outdated political ideology, but expressed by ordinary Irish people with a longing not to let go of the traditions and beliefs of their parents and grandparents. The government were talking European Union and the first computer in Ireland began operating in Shannon Airport.

For once, we have an account of things not going so well and during that year's Jurys season, Albert apparently told Goodliffe of a near disaster at one of the performances. It seems he had acquired a new trick whereby a magnet is clipped under a finger ring on the hand.

Albert had to buy a slightly oversized finger ring to accommodate the magnet. The ring was at best a cheap item after playing around with it, he promptly put it back in his jacket pocket and thought no more about it. In his stage show, Albert featured the Himber Linking Finger Rings which is a stunning baffler at the best of times but in Albert's hands it became a real miracle. A quick prop check before he went on stage, with a tap making sure he had the Himber Ring in his pocket and into the spotlight he appeared. It was only when the ring was positioned under a hanky on the magic wand held by the spectator and him reaching in his pocket for the Himber Ring did he realise that he was in trouble. The ring in his pocket was just the simple Woolworths article and sadly, he had to abandon the trick. Even after a thousand performances, it can happen even to the seasoned pro. But all was not lost. As the saying goes 'what goes around comes around' and that year at the all-Ireland convention, Albert received the America Trophy from Sam Mercer.

Christmas was a family time with a few special performances and quality family time. As this book is essentially a record of Albert le Bas' life as a magician in the public eye, it may appear as though magic was his only passion. This is not so. He was foremost a family man and there was not a day he was not there while we grew up. He taught us – albeit very badly, how to roller-skate. He was involved at every level in our school life and bless him, annually, he made a mess of Betty's immaculate kitchen oven-drying and sorting autumnal leaves in preparation for the hibernation of Tommy (our tortoise), who was snugly packed into a large leaf-filled box every October and placed among the summer fruits on the drying racks in the garage.

He remained ever besotted and in love with Betty. As her multiple sclerosis advanced, it became a struggle for her to go upstairs and move freely about the house. There came a time when it was easier for her to use a wheelchair when going out. This was a watershed and a very distressing time for Betty. There was still no valid treatment to arrest the spread of her illness. Occasionally there were 'snake oil' cures, hailed with great excitement among MS sufferers, but these resulted in little progress. There were various fad diets, when we all ate a huge amount of seaweed because the iron in it was thought to be good for disorders of the nervous system, or at another time everything cooked was gluten free or mostly prepared from sunflower seeds and tasted disgusting.

In the end, reality had to be faced. With heavy hearts, Betty and Albert decided that their home in Ballsbridge was no longer appropriate and they had to move. The search was on and once again, they took to house hunting – only this time accompanied by three children, who after a relatively short period of time became bored with weekend drives that only involved house viewing with not a sniff of a run on a beach or a Teddy's ice cream! There were several contenders for a new single level home, including the opportunity to design your own home in a development called 'The Coppings', close to Foxrock village and a beautiful, but isolated cottage called 'Pipers Croft' in the same locality. Eventually they settled on a four-bedroom bungalow set in a third of an acre in the suburb of Monkstown, South County Dublin.

Before the final decision on a new home was made, Albert had the wonderful opportunity to go to Stuttgart, Germany to appear at the USO American Bases. It seems the contract demanded that he had to do three shows a night. Albert had done that many times before in three different locations. Having heard about the conditions and the reaction of the troops, he was a little worried, but it all proved unfounded as he was (not surprisingly) a huge success! Accommodation was pre-arranged, and Albert found himself sharing a hotel room with the lads from Emmet Spiceland; an Irish folk band formed when brothers Brian and Michael Byrne of The Spiceland Folk Group joined forces with Donal Lunny and Mick Moloney. These were the new face of a revived Irish Folk scene and their performances amongst the American troops went down well. On a separate note, as a usually private and meticulously neat and tidy man, Albert came home to Betty with tales of a less-than-clean shared room, littered with beer bottles and unwashed clothes! Among the Irish artists were singers Pat and Jean, who gave a terrific performance as always.

Chris writes: "In April of that year and to honour Goodliffe, there was a Flying Sorcerers Convention in Jersey, Channel Islands. Sadly, due to work commitments in Germany, Albert couldn't come but in a letter of apology he wrote to Goodliffe thanking him for everything. To gain some additional publicity for that convention, I decided to use a brilliant idea of Albert's that he had used many years earlier in Dublin, whereby I took out an insurance policy in case the hotel 'vanished' during the convention period. I still have the policy! Naturally the publicity worked and there was a full house for the gala show. Thanks to the ingenuity of Albert, I had no need to claim on the policy!

Once again that year, Albert accepted a contract from Jurys hotel and committed to yet another long season.

In August 1968, Albert and Betty moved to their new family home in Monkstown, County Dublin, a quiet suburb a few minutes from the seafront at Dun Laoghaire and within easy reach of a bus and train system. The new house was in a cul de sac guarded at the entrance by the 13th Century ruin of a monk's monastery. It was a bungalow surrounded by about ten similar bungalows on one side of a large private green. It was perfect. There was no hoo-ha or special mention of Betty's change of circumstances. It was just accepted that from the day we moved into Monkstown, Betty now used a wheelchair all the time. It was the same but different. Same Mum, same rules, but Mum was now sitting down.

Betty and Albert loved that house and from the start, Betty's passion for colour and design kicked in. I have to say, never a gardener, Albert was perhaps a bit daunted by the prospect of maintaining the grounds, which included a rather large back garden which sloped right up to the wire fence of the Monkstown Lawn Tennis Club. He tackled the lawn mowing for a while using a Flymo mower attached to a long rope and starting at the top of the hill dropping it down to cut the grass and then pulling it back up. Not sure how long this ingenious solution lasted but within a short time, we miraculously had a gardener who tended the lawns beautifully. This move was disruptive for the entire family. The reason for the momentous move went mostly unmentioned – that it was to accommodate Betty's decline.

In a touching piece around this time, and following another visit to Dublin, Goodliffe himself wheelchair bound with MS at this time, wrote in *Abra* magazine:

"People may think I don't care about other people's problems, but this isn't so. Magicians are my friends and when they are sad, then I am sad. I wish it wasn't – it would be a lot less heart-breaking to stand aloof and look on these things with a dispassionate eye."

Christmas Time

Many people remember their childhood Christmas' as magical. As a child in a household that revolved around all things magical, our Christmas season took those experiences and subsequent memories to a different level.

December to January was a fantastic time. The Society of Irish Magicians (SIM) children's party was a start. I remember feeling so excited for the afternoon. It was usually held in a Dublin hotel. There were presents, streamers, balloons, party food and then a great show by the magicians. My sisters and I would be dressed in our Christmas outfits – new clothes from probably Newels on Grafton Street. This shop I remember well because it had a beautiful rocking horse you could ride on.

At the party, if you were lucky you could be asked up on stage to be an assistant and become part of the excitement. I have a picture of myself from the *Evening Press* newspaper in 1964 aged four at the SIM party, looking totally mesmerised. I love this photo.

As an aside, many years later when Dublin Magician Neville Wiltshire visited his daughter in Sydney and came to my house for lunch, he came as all magicians do, with his bag of tricks. I could hardly wait for lunch to be over as I knew what was coming and it had been so long since I had seen any magic. Neville did not disappoint! My children were adults at the time and alternated between hilarity and bafflement. Yvonne's son Finn was nine years old and the look on his face was of sheer delight – a look I knew well and treasured. I have to say Alma's husband Alex, who had never been exposed to magic before was equally enthralled and delighted. For me, this sums up what magic is all about.

But I digress…

Christmas in Ireland is often cold and damp and grey with snow. It is dark in the mornings when you rise and dark again by four pm. Weather aside, every year just before Christmas, we travelled as a family to what is proclaimed as the highest village in Ireland, Anamoe in County Wicklow, because every year a friend of Albert's held a Christmas party for all the local children in his home. His friend was Mr Robert Barton and his lovely wife Rachel.

It was always a great day. It was a big old house. A party and a show were held in a large reception room to the left of the front door. Albert would perform and sometimes I would help him, feeling very important holding a silver cannister that I knew on his cue would produce several wriggling snakes or ribbons, feeling a bit special I suppose.

But it was after the party was over, when the grand room was empty of children, strewn with balloons and streamers that the best part of the day would come. As evening fell, we would have dinner with Robert and Rachel in a large dining room, seated at a big mahogany table that seated perhaps twenty people. All decorated with china and crystal and made festive with holly, ivy and burning candles. The staff would serve us a delicious meal. After dessert, Robert would lead us to the enormous wall of wood and glass display cabinets that ran along one side of the room. There he would show us his treasures and give each of us a Christmas present with our names on it. I have to say the presents were often strange. I remember on one occasion. Yvonne received a set of miniature chandeliers for a dolls house that actually lit up. This might not excite any child today but in the 1960s, it was a bit special. That year I received a folded silk square heavily embroidered by some craftsman in the Far East. I still have it.

One special memory of this annual visit to the Barton's home was Mrs Barton taking me by the hand and handing me a small dusty box about the size of a matchbox that they had acquired on their travels in South America. Then she handed me a large magnifying glass with a long black handle to look at the contents. Inside were a pair of dressed fleas – a tiny bride and groom! To this day I have not seen anything like it except perhaps on a David Attenborough documentary.

During Albert's final months, Robert was often in contact with Betty and after Albert died, he wrote her many times. He had lost his beloved Rachel around the same time and I think they shared their grief in those letters. It was only years later as an adult that I came to learn that Robert was an important figure in Irish history.

His home 'Glendalough House' in Anamoe, Wicklow is considered one of the grandest stately homes in Ireland. He himself was an Irish nationalist politician elected to the British House of Commons. He was arrested in 1919 for sedition but escaped Mountjoy Prison, leaving a note for the governor requesting he keep his luggage until he sent for it! Along with Michael Collins, he was one of the signatories on the Anglo-Irish Treaty signed in London in December 1921, providing the establishment of the Irish Free State.

He was elected twice more and was appointed the first Minister of Agriculture of the Irish Republic. He eventually retired from politics for the law, practicing as a barrister and then a judge. As children, we knew him as a fascinating kindly old man with a house full of rare oddities and wonderful treasures.

For a few years, we spent the actual three days of Christmas in the Tower Hotel in Waterford. They ran a Christmas program which Dad emceed. It was not a disadvantage not to be home for Christmas as Santa came to us there too. On Christmas Eve night, there would be a gala dinner and a show. We would be dressed in our special evening dresses. Betty would look stunning in a slim fitting taffeta gown with jewels sparkling on her wrist and neck. Albert would be in a tuxedo for the night. The dinner was memorable because after the main meal the lights in the ballroom would be dimmed and a stream of waiters would circle the room each holding a flaming plum pudding. Albert's spot always went down well. At the end of the evening, us tired and happy kids would return to the hotel bedrooms where Santa (from the hotel) had already arrived and a wrapped present would be on our pillows. On Boxing Day, we would go to nearby Tramore to see off the hunt. For me who was 'horse mad', this was an exciting finish to the Christmas season with huge horses, fat huntsmen in their red jackets, yapping hounds and the unfamiliar sound of the bugle call.

The first year the family moved to Monkstown in 1968, Albert brought home a new artificial Christmas tree. Up until then we always had a real pine Christmas tree and Betty, who was so house proud, always bemoaned the fact that she was still vacuuming up pine needles in March. I suppose this was Albert's solution. At the time, imitation trees were getting popular, but they were mostly bright green and shiny in a very plastic sort of way. Our new tree was an eight-foot-tall gold tree that Albert had purchased from a display company. Nothing in our home was ever quite normal! Nevertheless, it did the job, fitted well with the late 60s décor and best of all, the Santa presents were under it on December 25th.

Childhood Christmas' spent at home bring memories of the smell of thyme, Betty hanging up the fresh turkey for a day before Christmas and setting up the dining room with all the Christmas fare. There was the annual expedition into the garage, a place that never had a car parked in it, but instead was home to Albert's illusions and racks of fruit picked from the garden in autumn and stored in the cool air. We ventured in to find the ham pot – a gigantic pot that Betty had bought at a house auction and which had to be cleaned of cobwebs in readiness for the leg of ham which would simmer away merrily while we went to Mass on Christmas morning. On December 26th, St Stephens Day, we would visit Uncle Ronnie, Aunt Alice and our cousins in Rathgar and have Christmas dinner all over again.

A notable event from 1968 was that Albert had decided it would be his last season with Jurys and in October that year, he bid a sad farewell to his companions in the show. Perhaps his decision was not all based on furthering his magical opportunities. Betty was increasingly in need of assistance at times, and Albert was determined not to be locked into an extended contract of seven nights a week. The management of Jurys hosted a wonderful goodbye party for him, and a beautifully engraved silver cigarette box was presented to Albert as a thank you for all his years of hard work.

The freedom of a summer where he could pick and select engagements was not lost on the family. We had summer holidays that were actually in the summer! Most years we went on holidays as a family somewhere in Ireland. I have a vague memory as a young child staying in my grandparent's summer place in Bettystown. A few black and white photos of those days remain.

As our lives were action-packed, holidays took on a more serene pace. A farmhouse in Killarney or lazy days in Parknasilla overlooking the beautiful Kenmare Bay in County Kerry, where Albert and Betty would relax and read while us children would run wild and indulge in our favourite pastime of eating all the little of dishes of peanuts set out for guests in the lounge area. As Albert was a lifelong tee teetotaller and Betty would only have a small sherry at Christmas time, our evenings were family occasions, playing cards, chatting and sometimes learning a few tricks.

By far, the family's favourite holiday spot was Ballymaloe in County Cork. An Irish Chef by the name of Myrtle Allen lived there on a five-hundred-acre farm with Ivan her husband. In 1964, she opened the lower rooms of her big stone farmhouse to become a restaurant called the Yeats Room and sometime after that, she took a small number of guests into the upper bedrooms.

With Betty's reduced mobility, it was too difficult for her to negotiate the inside stairs to the guest rooms, so we always stayed in the single level gate lodge which was also converted into guest accommodation. It was the affectionately known as 'The Mousehole'. I wonder if it still is?

There, Albert could tend to Betty's needs at her own pace. It was a typical quaint stone building with a half door and big fireplace. All our meals were eaten in the Yeats Room and we filled our days lazing by the pool, visiting the farm animals or horse riding. Ballymaloe is set in the beautiful village of Shanagarry which to our delight had a local potter that we visited just across the road, to sit in awe and watch the potter craft beautiful pieces all finished in his signature glazes the colours of autumn nuts and golden wheat. The last time we stayed in Ballymaloe was the summer of 1971. I think by that time, the restaurant had a Michelin star and Myrtle's daughter-in-law, Darina Allen, was beginning to become involved in running the restaurant. She would go on to become a well-known television chef and author. These were very happy days.

It was not that Albert slowed down after his epic run with Jurys Hotel, just that he was more selective. In April 1969, he compèred the Ring 85 convention in the Royal Hotel, Bray.

1969 was a year tinged with sadness as his delightful mother Josephine le Bas passed away in June of that year. She was buried in the le Bas family plot in Mount Jerome cemetery, Dublin. After her death, his father Samuel, became a more frequent visitor arriving each week for tea with his little poodle and always hiding three bars of chocolate under his hat which he left on the hall table. I think he was a lonely man. Albert was always delighted to see him, and 'Pop' was always welcome.

Albert maintained a whirlwind pace throughout 1970 and 1971. In April 1970, we all travelled to the Slieve Donard Hotel in Newcastle, County Down, Northern Ireland. There, the Ulster Society of Magicians played host to the combined Magical Societies SIM and Ring 85. Albert performed and again, wowed his peers with a rapid rendition of The Misers Dream. This was a troubling period in Irish history with sectarian violence erupting in the six counties, but magic is a unifying craft and the convention was a huge success. An added bonus for us children was again, access to UK lollies and clothing that were still unavailable in the Republic. Later in the year, Albert compèred the Dana concert in the National Stadium.

Betty meanwhile, concentrated on their home and the girls. She accompanied Albert on every possible occasion, although many venues at that time were not wheelchair accessible.

In April 1971, they travelled again to London, this time not for a convention but for a rather special event. They were guests at the wedding of the amazing young Magician Chris Woodward to his beautiful bride the lovely Nadine Fogel, daughter of legendary magician Maurice Fogel. It was a memorable occasion at the Dorchester Hotel in London. Whilst the young bride looked stunning, so too did Betty in a newly made short turquoise dress. Betty was never one to lose sight of current fashion trends. I'm not sure what on your calendar could compete with this stylish wedding but later that year, Albert had a very successful couple of weeks hosting the summer cabaret in the Royal Marine Hotel in Dun Laoghaire. As usual this was written up in *Abra Magazine* by Goodliffe:

"This location would be at least five minutes from his nearby home and apart from the props, he could probably walk to the job! This season continues until September when he goes to Tralee for another season for a week. This was the Festival of Kerry which has now grown to world-wide recognition as 'The Rose of Tralee', an erstwhile beauty pageant attracting young women of Irish heritage from all corners of the globe, where the emphasis is not at all on appearances but rather on wholesomeness and traditional values held.

Albert was then back at the Intercontinental Hotel in Dublin for a month-long engagement… it would be tedious of me to say again that I have never met a more entertaining magician or one more deserving of the non-stop round of engagements which come his way. So, I'll skip that!"

He was, however, pleased to learn that Albert had been booked to appear at The Magic Circle banquet on October 16th at The Café Royal in London's West End with fellow artist and friend, Maurice Fogel. He reported that both scored well and Albert 'raced through his tried and tested material of the Misers Dream, Snake Basket, Linking Fingers and Balloon Giraffe at high speed in the professional style that only comes from constant performance'.

Following this event, Albert received a lovely letter of congratulations from the President of the Magic Circle, Mr John Salisse. This letter has survived and was treasured, a testimony to the fact that praise from his fellow magicians was very special indeed.

Albert was getting restless, his tried and tested acts like the Misers Dream and various card tricks, although always crowd pleasers, were becoming tired and he needed something new and exciting to present to his audience. It was time once again to revisit the spectacle of a large illusion. His answer came in the form of the 'Zig Zag Girl'.

Although perhaps equally famous for his Origami books and consequent TV series, in 1970 English magician and inventor Robert Harbin, wrote a long-awaited magic book simply called *Magic of Robert Harbin*. It contained all the wonderful items that he had invented and performed over the many years of his illustrious career. The one long-awaited gem amongst all of them was the Zig Zag Girl. This was a stage illusion akin to the more famous 'Sawing a woman in half'. In the zigzag illusion, the magician divides his assistant into thirds, only to have them emerge at the end of the illusion unharmed.

Harbin had actually invented it in 1965 and it has been hailed as one of the greatest illusions ever invented due to the impossibility of the trick and the fact that unlike many illusions, it can be performed surrounded by spectators.

In the production, the magician presents a life-sized box on which is painted the outline of a woman. The box is clearly in three sections, with the top portion having a hole where the assistants face protrudes. In the middle section, there is a small door that can be opened to reveal the assistant's tummy and an opening where her right hand sticks out and waves. In the third section, the outline is of the legs with another opening where the right foot protrudes, and the toes can wriggle and be felt.

The magic happens when the magician inserts a blade between the top section and the mid-section and another blade dissecting the midsection from the lower legs and foot. At all times the assistant's face, hand, stomach and foot are clearly visible and moving. With the help of an assistant from the audience, they are authenticated. The magician then runs the blades through the sections and slowly pushes the whole midsection to one side, sliding her tummy way out to the left and revealing a girl in an apparently impossible dissected zigzag position. It is truly a spectacular illusion.

Owners of Harbin's book were granted permission to build or have built, the Zig Zag Girl. This book contained the instructions on how to perform the illusion. The book was limited to 500 copies worldwide. At the time it was the most expensive magical book ever sold. Of course, Albert had to have it. He did purchase the book in late 1971 and commissioned the illusion to be built.

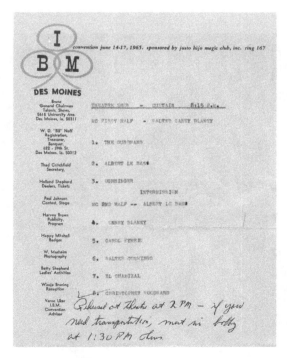

Abracadabra THE WORLD'S ONLY MAGICAL WEEKLY

EDITED BY GOODLIFFE

15 Booth Street Birmingham 21 England

KNOWLE 2110 NOR 9255

4th June 1965

Mr.C.Woodward,
Pinewood,
Les Ruisseaux St.
BRELADES BAY,
JERSEY.C.I.

Dear Christopher,

Detailed itinerary is as follows:-

12 June Flight TW 771 Dep.London 12.30 Arr.Chicago 15.10
  "   " UA 779   " Chicago 17.05 " Des Moines 17.40
18 June " UA 880   " Des Moines 12.05 Arr.Chicago 15.04
23 "   " NW 433   " Chicago 10.20 " Milwaukee 10.46
27 "   " NW 312   " Milwaukee 16.10 " Detroit 17.05
27 "   " AA 912   " Detroit 18.15 " Buffalo 20.27
29 "   " MO 212   " Buffalo 17.10 " New York 19.14
29 "   " TW 708   " New York 22.15 " London 09.50
                                        (30 June)

The cost is £207.4.0 per head a little more than
estimated because some of the flights are first
class only.

Sincerely yours,

G.

G/do

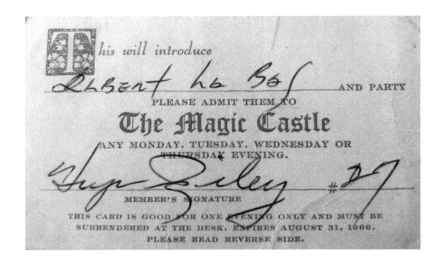

Oofle Dust

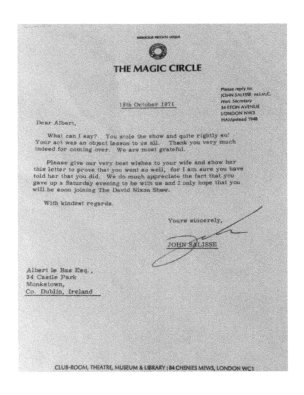

THE MAGIC CIRCLE

18th October 1971

Please reply to:
JOHN SALISSE, M.I.M.C.
Hon. Secretary
34 ETON AVENUE
LONDON NW3
HAMpstead 1948

Dear Albert,

What can I say? You stole the show and quite rightly so! Your act was an object lesson to us all. Thank you very much indeed for coming over. We are most grateful.

Please give our very best wishes to your wife and show her this letter to prove that you went so well, for I am sure you have told her that you did. We do much appreciate the fact that you gave up a Saturday evening to be with us and I only hope that you will be soon joining The David Nixon Show.

With kindest regards.

Yours sincerely,

JOHN SALISSE

Albert le Bas Esq.,
34 Castle Park
Monkstown,
Co. Dublin, Ireland

CLUB-ROOM, THEATRE, MUSEUM & LIBRARY : 84 CHENIES MEWS, LONDON WC1

MAGIC CIRCLE 65
SUBJECT TO ALTERATION WITHOUT NOTICE

MICHAEL BAILEY will introduce the artistes

"WHO'S WHO?" ... ... devised by Gerald Holgate	YURI GRIDNEFF & Partner ... The juggling unicyclist
JOHN WADE ... ... The Patter of Magic Feats	ARTHUR POLLARD ... ... Almost a magician
ALICE ... ... The enchanting magicienne	ALBERT LE BAS ... ... Ireland's leading magician
PEGGY & JULIA PALETTE ... "The Pictures who Paint"	
SINO ... ... The Magic Top Hat Parade	TONNY van DOMMELEN ... "The Dream of a Croupier"
SAMSON ... ... Denmark's novelty magician	ARNO & RITA van BOLEN ... The International Deceivers

INTERVAL 15 MINUTES

JACK WALKER and his orchestra

Direction	MICHAEL BAILEY
Administration...	NORMAN COOPER
Production	GIL LEANEY
Box Office Manager	GEORGE FARROW
Stage Manager	BERNARD LOVETT
Asst. Stage Manager	JOHN NAPIER
Stage Staff ... ... David Hill, Richard Saunders, Keith Cooper	

LICENSING REGULATIONS. In accordance with the requirements of the Lord Chamberlain:— 1.—The public may leave at the end of all performances by all exit doors and such doors must at that time be open. 2.—All gangways, passages and staircases must be kept entirely free from chairs or any other obstructions. 3.—Persons shall not in any circumstances be permitted to stand or sit in any of the gangways intersecting the seating, or to sit in any of the other gangways. If standing be permitted in the gangways at the sides and rear of the seating it shall be strictly limited to the number indicated in the notices exhibited in those positions. 4.—The safety curtain must be lowered and raised in the presence of each audience.

Taking pictures in the Auditorium is prohibited.

107

Barbara le Bas

Iuductio Potestas Lagus

THE MAGIC CIRCLE

Annual Banquet, Cabaret and Dance

FRANCIS WHITE, Esq., M.I.M.C.
President of the Magic Circle

Saturday, 16th October, 1965
Café Royal, London, W.I.

Menu	Toasts
Coupe de Melon Jubilée	HER MAJESTY THE QUEEN
*	Proposed by the President
Délice de Sole François Blanc	
*	*
Contrefilet de Bœuf Bordelaise	
Petits Pois au Beurre	THE MAGIC CIRCLE
Pommes Croquettes	
*	Proposed by Peter Jones Esq.,
Soufflé Magic Circle	Response by Francis White, Esq., M.I.M.C.
Petits Fours	who will propose the toast to our Guests
*	Responses by J. B. Priestley, Esq., M.A., LL.D., D.Litt.
Café	Cyril Fletcher, Esq.

The Jubilee Cabaret

ALBERT LE BAS　　　　　　　　　　　SYD MARX

WALLACE, DELYSE AND TWO JEANETTES

Billy McComb	Geoffrey Robinson	John Salisse
Leslie Press	Percy Press	George Wallihan
David Budd	Patrick Page	Jack Rowlands
Ronald Bridges	Anthony Crabbe	Alan Shaxon
	ROBERT HARBIN	

Production specially devised and produced by
PHIL BURN

108

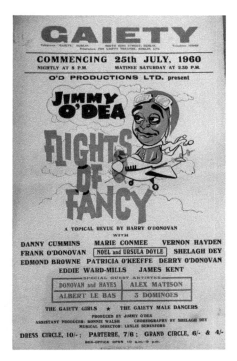

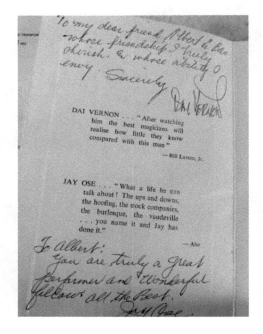

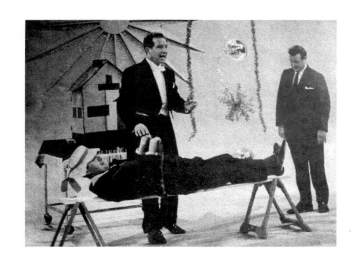

SCENE 5

The Final Curtain

After a rollercoaster ride for thirty years, chasing the dream and building castles in the air, we come to 1972. There is a lot in Albert's 'achieved' pile and a huge amount in his 'yet to do' pile.

Ireland is growing and booming with President Eamon De Valera at the helm and the Fianna Fáil government is led by Taoiseach Jack Lynch, who on Jan 22nd signed the Treaty of Accession to the European Union. Sadly, this momentous event in Irish history was overshadowed just eight days later on January 30th by the terrible events of Bloody Sunday. On this day, thirteen unarmed civilians were shot dead in Derry as British soldiers opened fire on a banned civil rights march.

Removed from national politics, life was good in Monkstown, Betty's condition had remained stable for some time. That is not to say there were limitations. Now fully confined to a wheelchair, Betty's mobility was severely restricted but her upper body strength had not yet faded, and she could transfer independently giving her some dignity in personal care. Her mind was as sharp as ever. Thankfully, the MS never affected her speech. She had connected with the MS Society and whilst their intentions were good, she was not that receptive to the well-intentioned visitors who came to chat and give support. In many ways, her life experiences were so detached from the stories they shared that she dreaded those impromptu visits from the 'cucumber sandwich brigade' and preferred to concentrate on setting her own home right.

The girls were doing well at school with friends and hobbies to get involved in. Barbara was now at school in Sion Hill and Louise, still at Rockford Manor, was preparing for a major exam. Nine-year-old Yvonne was happily doing what carefree nine-year-olds do. On the entertainment front, Albert was more in demand than ever with appearance fees to match. All in all, life was good. The roses, albeit with a few scattered thorns, were still coming.

The Zig Zag arrived at our home in Monkstown in huge packing cases – brought into the country by Trevor Lewis on the ferry. It was duly assembled in the living room.

There is a short aside here concerning a transgression which I fessed up to after many years to Neville Wiltshire.

As a background, with all illusions, tricks and magical apparatus in our home, there was an accepted understanding that as a child, you did not touch anything – ever – and of course being children, we did. In the past, I have opened a dove pan and released a stream of multicoloured ribbons that had been carefully ironed and prepared by Betty for a forthcoming show or dislodged some flash paper or upset a thumb nail loaded with chemicals, but children will be children…

Within a day of the Zig Zag being assembled in the sitting room, I ventured in to investigate and try it out. In so doing, I caused a crack in one of the doors. Albert had not yet had the time to fully explore the unit. When he did so the next evening, he discovered this crack to his dismay. He immediately arranged for that section to be sent back and remade. I admit I was in my late forties before I fessed up to being responsible – a fact that was written up by Neville Wiltshire in the SIM magazine in 2010.

In 1971, this was the biggest illusion since The Substitution that Albert was preparing to present. As Betty was no longer his assistant and he had now spent many years working solo, he needed an assistant. Louise was fifteen at that point. She was slim, dark haired, quiet, self-contained and stunningly beautiful like her mother. While growing up, she had assisted in the act as a child and was familiar with dressing in theatrical costumes. She had successfully performed the Dolls House illusion in the past. She was looking like the ideal candidate.

But girls of fifteen are shy, self-conscious and crave the ordinary, wanting to be like their peers going to school, playing tennis and reading teenage magazines. Louise was not inherently attention-seeking and while it was a novelty to have appeared on stage in various shows and on television as a younger child, strutting on stage as a mature 'magicians assistant' in a short flashy costume was on a different level and presented a different challenge. Whether she was willing or had to be talked into it, ultimately, she agreed.

In preparation for her role, Albert arranged for Louise to complete a training course with Betty Whelan. She was a former Irish international model who was now offering training for young ladies in deportment, make up and 'presence'. It was arranged that Louise attend private sessions with Betty Whelan in the Royal Marine Hotel, which she duly did. Betty le Bas took charge of the new assistant's costume and after many discussions, the outfit was agreed on – a pale pink very short skater type dress with a high neckline circled with sparkling silver trimming, blue and silver shimmering tights (which were bought from London) and silver sequined slippers. Louise was transformed, albeit reluctantly, into a 'show girl' and the plans progressed. Of course, there was countless nights of rehearsal at home where every word, look and movement were practiced until they were perfect. In hindsight, it must have been a challenging time for Louise who was studying at that time for her Intermediate Certificate exams, a mandatory academic achievement in Irish secondary (High School) education.

Together, Albert and his new assistant Louise premiered their new illusion at the Royal Marine Hotel in Dun Laoghaire and the reception was amazing. In September 1971, they took the act to County Kerry, performing at the Rose of Tralee Festival at Ashe Memorial Hall. It was a stage built in front of the hall so the whole show was outdoors.

Along with singers Jack O'Connor and Marjorie Courtney, they stayed in Fenit and took in the Tralee horse races during their stay.

RTE, the national television and broadcasting agency in Ireland, soon got wind of this new spectacular act and engaged Albert to be the intermission performer for the 8th National Song Contest in February 1972. A gig which Albert readily accepted. He was confident with his new illusion. It was time to expose it to a broader audience.

By way of explanation for readers not familiar with the enormity of this gig; each year in the 1970s, Ireland as a nation, submitted a song to the European Song Contest. Now called Eurovision. It was based on the San Remo Music Festival held in Italy in 1951. It is a song contest that has been broadcast on European television since 1956, making it the longest running television program in the world and one of the most popular non-sporting events watched with audiences between 100 and 600 million. As a pre-cursor to the actual competition, each country holds a national song contest to select the song that will best represent their county. In most competing countries, this is a highly anticipated and much watched TV program. Ireland was no exception. It is perhaps hard to explain the enormity and popularity of this event. There was probably not a home in Ireland that did not tune in and watch.

It was the perfect platform to offer a new and astounding illusion to the Irish people, and it was also a first for a magical act of international calibre to be showcased.

Albert was ready. Louise was ready. The TV program was due to be broadcast to approximately three million Irish viewers live from the Cork Opera House. Rehearsals began the day before. The host of the show was TV personality Mike Murphy. The twelve hopeful singers assembled with their musicians to compete for the honour of performing the song to represent their country. The TV show was due to be broadcast live on Sunday 13th February. Albert and Louise set off from Monkstown, both nervous and excited in their own way. They stayed in the Metropole Hotel in Cork and partook in the day-long rehearsal before the live performance.

The rehearsals appeared to be a tiring time for Albert, his usual energy and enthusiasm off stage was absent. On stage he was ever the polished performer. Louise in a phone call home to Betty reported that after the second day of rehearsals, Albert took to his bed in the hotel for a rest in the afternoon – an action unheard of, he had chills and a small nose bleed.

The live filming and broadcast were a huge success, slick and professional, the hopeful songsters were expertly introduced and welcomed by Mike Murphy. While the judges made their decisions, the intermission act of Albert and Louise wowed and baffled audiences in the Cork Opera house and around the country. It was perhaps one of Albert's most engaging and polished performances. He was word and action perfect. His music score was brilliant with Louise walking on stage to the strains of *Every little breeze seems to whisper Louise*. Then the performance gained momentum as the illusion progressed.

Louise was fantastic, every bit the professional and beguiling assistant. There was nothing about the performance that could have been improved. It was a triumph of magical performances!

Albert and Louise skipped the afterparty, and left after congratulating the deserved winner, Sandy Jones on her winning song *Ceoil an Grá*, which means the music of love. This was the first time Ireland had selected a song in its native Gaelic language.

They retired in the hotel where Albert fell into an exhausted sleep in readiness for his drive back to Dublin the following day.

It was to be his last ever performance.

Arriving back home on the Monday, Betty immediately saw that something was not quite right, that Albert was unwell. She arranged for an appointment with the local doctor that afternoon who diagnosed the flu. The following day, feeling increasingly fatigued, he sought a second opinion from a long-time trusted medical friend, a specialist called Dr

Phil Brennan. Dr Brennan immediately decided that Albert was a very sick man and arranged admission to Saint Vincent's Hospital in Elm Park, Dublin on that very same day.

Over the coming days in hospital, Albert was subjected to a battery of tests and scans. By the end of the week, the news was not good. The diagnosis was frightening. He had Acute Myeloid Leukaemia. He was formally admitted under Haematologist, Dr Liam O'Connell.

Albert was forty-four years old.

Leukaemia is a cancer of blood-forming tissues, including bone marrow. It is still not clear today what causes leukaemia but is thought to involve a combination of genetic and environmental factors. Leukaemia cells have acquired mutations in their DNA that cause them to grow abnormally and lose typical white blood cell functions. It was not until 1974 that there was a development in leukaemia treatment with the introduction of cytarabine to induce remission. Two years too late for Albert.

Albert's and Betty's life, their home life and of course, their children's lives took on a new change and a new challenge. Although confined to a wheelchair, Betty was still driving. Her little red Mini was fitted with a Feeney and Johnston hand control. From the first day of his admission, as a family, we began the nightly trips from Monkstown into Ballsbridge to visit Albert.

A new routine developed in our home. The children did their homework and studies when they arrived home at 4pm, they helped prepare dinner and ate it. Then at 6.30pm each night, all of us would pile into Betty's Mini, load her wheelchair into the boot and we would drive to St Vincent's Hospital in time for evening visiting at 7pm.

When he was in isolation during extreme treatment or times when his resistance to infection was low, Albert would wait for us at the top window of the fourth floor in St Vincent's. When we pulled into the hospital complex, he would be there in his fawn dressing gown at the window, waving to us. These were good evenings when you knew he had a good day and had the strength to walk the long corridor of St Patricks ward.

We did not really understand. Louise was sixteen, I was fourteen and Yvonne just nine years old. Together, we trooped into the ward seven nights a week. Usually he was in good form and delighted to see us. He would often have made a small origami figure for each of us or secretly pass us a sealed letter telling us how proud he was when he heard we had done well in a test or achieved some other minor school accolade. I have a letter from him saying how proud he was of an apple tart I had baked. Trying I suppose, to remain involved in the everyday life and challenges of his children.

Sometimes, we would leave Albert and Betty alone to have a chat and we would go downstairs to the main hospital foyer and visit the hospital shop and secretively buy sweets. It was in this giant foyer that Betty encountered two former neighbours from St Albans Park, both of their husbands were receiving treatment at that time in the same hospital. Mrs Mullins our next-door neighbour in Ballsbridge was forlorn and distressed because her husband had some illness – I don't know what it was. Mrs Aunger whose house had been opposite to ours, was tearful and explained that her beloved husband had suffered a stroke. On the occasions Betty met with these women, by accident, in the sterile vast foyer of St Vincent's, they all discussed funerals and black suits and how to cope as potential widows with the seriousness of their current situation. In the end, it was only Betty who bought a black suit that year.

New important figures were introduced into our young lives that year. Not least a truly caring and gentle nun called Sister Paschal who was the Nurse Unit Manager of St Patrick's ward. I thought at the time she was old but in hindsight she was probably less than forty. She was a stern looking nun in a pristine habit and veil who extruded an air of absolute authority but whom I later realised was a most compassionate soul. I think she was of huge help to Betty at that time. Father Fox, the

Chaplin of St Vincent's, was an ambling gentle soul of perhaps fifty years, who had spent many years on the missions in Africa and whose caring and empathetic nature made him a favourite with Albert and Betty. His connection with our family at the time was again indicative of our parents' religious values and the role once again, that religion and belief played in their lives. Father Fox became a frequent visitor to our home during these months. Just a social call for a cup of tea where he would regale us with stories of his years in Africa, about the times when he went into the jungle and collected new born baby girls who were unwanted by their mothers because they were female, and placed them in an old wheelbarrow to bring them back to the mission house to be cared for.

After each nightly visit to the hospital, we had a routine. We drove home in Betty's Mini and were home by nine o'clock. Then before bed, together we would kneel in prayer in the sitting room and recite the prayer to St Jude, the patron saint of desperate situations and hopeless cases. I can still recite it word perfect...

"Most holy apostle, St Jude, faithful servant and friend of Jesus, the church honours and invokes you as the patron saint of hopeless cases, of matters despaired of. Pray for me, I am so helpless and alone. Intercede with God for me that he brings visible and speedy help where help is most despaired of. Come to my assistance in this great need that I may receive consolation and help of heaven in all my sufferings, please make Dad well again. I promise St Jude, to be ever mindful of this great favour granted me by God and to always honour you as a special and powerful patron, and to gratefully encourage devotion to you. Amen."

At the time, I am not sure that we, with perhaps the exception of Louise, were actually aware that our prayers were in the realm of hopeless cases.

In the end, St Jude did not actually come through for us.

During this time, ever-strong Betty soldiered on. There was not a day she was not up and in the kitchen in her wheelchair with breakfast ready and immaculate school uniforms to hand. How little we understood what she must have been going through. Yes, we were independent and questioning young girls but while Betty would have known the likely prognosis, it was not shared with us children. For many months, hope lived in our hearts as to the day that Dad would be home again.

And he did come home. In August, he came home for one night. Was it a compassionate visit allowed by the medical team because they knew what we did not? But oh, the excitement after six months! He was tired, thin and weak. I helped put him to bed that night. He was tearful and told me, "This is not what I thought it would be like to be home. I'm sorry, pet. It will be better next time." I helped take off his socks then sometime later he started vomiting blood and was taken back into St Vincent's the next day.

I have often wondered when grief begins because I am sure in cases of a terminal illness it is certainly not on the day of death, rather it is a slow process with tiny drops of hope dissolving as each day closes, with sorrow seeping in to fill their place. Was it like this for Betty? To her credit, there were very few times she broke down in front of us. Surely, she was wracked with the prospect of loss and the overwhelming fear of being a relatively young widow with three children and her own progressive illness to manage. I am at a loss to even imagine how you manage the prospect of losing your best friend and soul mate – the one you live for, laugh with and love, of them not being there. In hindsight, ever private and determinedly independent Betty probably did not share her deepest emotions or anxieties with anyone, except perhaps her mother. Granny Merriman became a more frequent visitor and stalwart of the family during Albert's hospitalisation. She would arrive on a Tuesday and stay until Friday night. In the late evening, one of us would walk her up Monkstown Avenue to catch the 46A bus back to

Donnybrook where she would spend the weekend in her own home, and return again the next week to support and help her daughter.

As for Albert, his years of being a gentle friend to his colleagues, both in and out of the entertainment world, came full circle. There was a steady stream of visitors, when allowed. Visiting UK magicians made the trip into the hospital to see him, his illness was mentioned in *Abra Magazine* and well wishes came from the magical community, both in Europe and America. There was a host of international wand-wielding sorcerers willing him to wellness.

Michael Slazenger of Powerscourt House who he had entertained at his 21st birthday and who was now himself a doctor in the hospital, often came to sit and chat. All those years later, he was still entertained by Albert's small collection of card tricks that he kept in the Formica bedside locker. In Dublin, his pals from Jurys came often. John Mc Nally visited almost nightly, bringing food like a beautiful memory of past days from the chef in Jurys, which was a lovely gesture, but sadly, Albert was often unable to eat. When not at the hospital, friends like Marjorie Courtney were with Betty in Monkstown offering support, coming in after a day's work, kicking off their shoes and having tea with a Teatime Express cake. In the background, Betty was realistic and working with an already shattered heart, was preparing for the worst.

Monday September 11th was like any other Monday. During our visit that night, we probably had stories of our weekend events and our anticipation of the banal school week ahead. Albert had been quite low that night and our visit was short. Betty spent an extra-long time alone in conversation with Sister Paschal who had, unusually, stayed back after her shift to talk to her. Father Fox was there too. Albert was in isolation again and very weak. We all gowned up in paper masks, voluminous paper gowns and gloves to enter the room. He was hardly talking but acknowledged each of us with a smile and a slight tightening of his thin but warm hard around ours. At the end of the short visit, Betty made sure we all kissed him goodnight.

Unbeknown to us, the final vigil had begun.

That night we drove home in silence. Our evening petition to Saint Jude seemed to be more earnest and tearful than ever.

Tuesday morning at eight am the phone rang. I was in the kitchen with Betty, who was going through the motions of breakfast and preparing school breaks. It was Sister Paschal. I wheeled Betty to the phone on the dining room table and ran immediately to Louise who was dressing for school, adjusting her green and gold stripped tie and preparing that day to receive the results of her Intermediate Examination results. I can vividly see her reflection as she stood in front of her long mirror as I said, "Sister Paschal is on the phone. I think it's Dad." We went to the dining room where Betty was holding a silent telephone receiver with tears running down her face. Albert had lost his battle at three am that morning.

His star, which has shone so bright both on stage and off for so many years, had flickered and dimmed. Just like that, he was gone.

That day was a flurry of activity and numbness, if that contradiction is possible. A day when grieving was postponed in order to attend to the processes and rituals of death.

Betty made the phone calls to Albert's heartbroken father, his brother Ronald, her own mother and family, relatives and friends. Each call becoming more and more distressing and heart wrenching. What an absolutely awful task for a grieving woman to have to do. I think perhaps her heart was irreplaceably ripped apart that day.

These were the days before instant communicating – no Facebook, mobile phones, Twitter or Instagram. Communication was by landline phone, letter or in urgent times, telegram. By late morning, the telegrams started arriving. In the end, there were hundreds and hundreds of them – from friends, family, businesses and magicians around the world. As the news travelled, the phone started ringing with heartfelt calls of condolences. One call I answered was from Jack Lynch the Irish Prime Minister offering his best wishes and kind thoughts.

Late that afternoon, just the four of us – Betty and her girls, set off once again on the twenty-minute journey to St Vincent's Hospital, a route we had become so familiar with over the preceding eight months. We had travelled it 240 times before and knew every twist and turn in the road, every speed bump and traffic light, but this time it was a different journey. There was an unspoken air of finality and sadness, a mist of numbness around each of us for which none of us had any words and no place to put the feelings, so, no one spoke. There were no jokes, no sibling snipes at each other, no commentary. We were subdued, emotionally drained, disbelieving and dazed.

On entering the St Vincent's hospital campus, we turned not this time towards the main entrance to access the foyer and the lift to St Patricks ward, but to an unknown quiet building, unfamiliar to us. There we were met by Sister Paschal and Father Fox and several other staff members of St Patricks ward unknown to me, but all in tears. We had arrived at the hospital morgue.

Here on a silver metal gurney, Albert was laid out in a white shroud. His arms folded gently on his chest and his hands entwined with a string of rosary beads. Sleeping forever. In her chair, Betty wheeled up to him. She was at face level with him. She lovingly held his head, stroked his cheek and silently cried like one whose heart was shattered. And it was.

She encouraged us all to touch him and say goodbye. I recall the coldness, the absolute shocking coldness of his clasped hands as I said my goodbyes. Those soft white hands, that had for nigh on thirty years manipulated tricks, confounded thousands with his gift of legerdemain and awed thousands of delighted strangers with their dexterity. Those gentle loving hands that had handled us with unconditional love and care as babies, as toddlers and young children, wiping away our tears blood and snot, stroking us to sleep, writing us messages of validation, teaching us tricks we would never master but delighted in the trying, and at all times, offering a safe, soothing and comforting space. They were so very still, so cold.

The next few days were a blur.

The neighbours and friends rallied around and brought with them gifts of food and what words of condolences they had. They did the best people can do in the face of a situation where there are no words.

Albert had accepted death. He got on with dying the same way he had got on with living, day by day, pressing forward, albeit ever hopeful. His life, a life lived out loud for so many years, was eventually shrunk to a small hospital room and I think he knew he would not see the end of the year.

How lucky we were that the community Albert had belonged to for so long was a community of artists and performers whose every day was a testimony to laughter and happiness. Consequently, visitors to our home in the following days were not solemn for long, sad condolences quickly morphed into recounting tales of good times, of great shows, of spectacular success and stories of thousands of happy audience members who for a short while, as Peter Mooney wrote, allowed Albert to 'Make again small children of their hearts'.

The entertainment community came and grieved, laughed out loud, talked and gossiped. They offered countless handshakes and 'Sorry for your troubles' utterances, all the while teaching us how to be brave and go on living, no matter how great the rupture or loss.

Albert's funeral was held, not in Monkstown where he had lived for just over three years, but in his former parish of Our Lady Queen of Peace Church in Merrion. It's a huge church with seating for seven hundred people and on the day of his funeral it was packed to capacity. I have no idea who helped Betty organise the service but, on the day, everything was just beautiful. The hymns were sung by baritone Edmund Brown and soprano Mary Sheridan sung a beautiful rendition of *Panis Angelicus*. There were few dry eyes in the congregation. Betty in her wheelchair, held her head up high, dressed in a new black suit and wearing the gold necklace Albert had given her for her birthday that year, remained dry eyed, stoic and watchful of her children.

Following the service, the funeral cortege travelled to Deans Grange Cemetery in Blackrock where somehow Betty had secured a burial plot on the main mature treelined avenue and where Albert was lowered to his final resting place to the quiet chant of farewell prayers.

The day was cold, and the wind whistled through the open space of the cemetery. Perhaps through exhaustion or overwhelming grief, Betty did not actually leave the large black mourning car that was parked at the graveside. Yvonne, too little for such a traumatic event, had been taken home by the Sherry's, kindly neighbours. Louise was in the loving shelter of Fionnula Nugent a good friend from St Alban's Park, standing beside the priest, among the mourners that had gathered for the final prayers.

I stayed in the back of the car with Betty, only venturing out when the main prayers were over, and the crowds began to disperse. I went out to lay a single flower on his grave and being alone, became quite overwhelmed. It was Mai Lambert that rescued me, held me to her ample bosom and brought me back to Mum. It is strange the things that you remember.

For a man who had craved publicity and write ups, Albert would not have been disappointed with the reaction to his passing.

A Broken Wand ceremony was held for him in the Magic Circle – the magicians tradition way of saying farewell to a fellow sorcerer. His obituary was mentioned in the US magazine, *The Linking Ring* Vol 52 issue no 11. It simply stated that Albert, membership no 20364, who had been performing for some thirty years in theatres and had appeared at the 1965 Des Moines Convention, had passed away.

There was also a simple obituary in *The Stage* Newspaper on September 21st page 7. In *Abra*, issue no 1391, the editor and long-time friend Goodlife greatly lamented the passing of Albert and wrote the following lengthy tribute to a wonderful friend:

Albert Le Bas 1928 – 1972

On Tuesday of last week after an illness lasting several months Albert Le Bas died in Dublin at the early age of 44. I lost a good friend, and magic lost one of its most outstanding entertainers.

Albert was an exuberant personality. Cheerful even in the face of adversity, he phoned me only quite recently to say that he was back home after a long spell in hospital and that he had lost a lot of weight. "If the door opens and nobody comes in, it's me!" he said. He did however add that he was eating like a horse and obviously expected that it would not be long before he was in action again. Unhappily is was not to be.

He was Ireland's premier magician. If there was a top date to be played either in the flesh or on TV, Albert was the first choice. Cautious, because he had a wife and three daughters, he never abandoned his day job with (Archers) a big Ford distributor, but he was lucky in that he was able to obtain considerable time off to fulfil his many dates. More than once when Princess Margaret was in the Republic of Ireland meeting her in-laws, Albert was the chosen entertainer. Countless thousands of American and other foreign visitors must have seen him working, season after season, at Jurys Hotel in Dublin. He appeared in Magic Circle and convention shows in this country and joined the last party of the Flying Sorcerers which I took to America where he scored the success he enjoyed everywhere else.

In front of me I have *Abra* #291 February 4th, 1950, which carries a report of the Irish Convention by Billy McComb. He says: 'Le Bas and Company brought their slick illusion act. Here's an up and coming performer scoring with different effects as different as The Dolls House and The Note in Cigarette. I was sorry that no official saw fit to mention this was his 22nd birthday.' From then on, our pages have followed his success year by year.

The tricks that he did were for the most part standard items. The Misers Dream, at tremendous speed with a child's seaside bucket, The Koran Linking Finger Rings which he did better than anyone else I ever saw present it. The Egg Bag using a glass of whisky. Albert was a lifelong teetotaller, so it wasn't really whisky in the glass. And several more readily portable easy-to-assemble, clean-cut straightforward items, all of which had been stripped of anything which tended to slow down the action and so confuse the issue. He made one balloon animal, a giraffe. In the manufacturing routine, he incorporated almost every known balloon gag in the book. It was a masterpiece of concentrated entertainment.

I could go on indefinitely relating anecdotes about Albert and sing his praises but that would become tedious and so would surely not please him. To his widow Betty and his daughters, *Abra* extends profound sympathy. They have the consolation that he will live in the memory of the vast numbers he entertained so consistently over a quarter of a century, packing more good magic into those years that most succeed in doing in twice that time.

Albert Le Bas' funeral took place on Thursday of last week. The church was packed. All the magicians from the Irish Republic attended, including Emile Swann this year's

president from the North. There were considerable numbers
from the theatre, circus and TV.

In Dublin too the entertainment community, not just magicians but
other artists who had shared the boards with this gentle artist over the years
were keen to do something to help. Under the guidance and production of
Fred O'Donovan, a memorial concert was arranged. The date was set for
Sunday October 22nd, 1972, in The Gaiety Theatre Dublin. The tickets for
the show were sold out within minutes of the announcement.

Before this, Betty had a trip to make. Months earlier both herself and
Albert had planned and booked a trip to Lourdes in France. Hopeful I
suppose that Albert would be well enough to undertake the journey. It was
a pilgrimage arranged by the Dublin Dioceses to the holy site of Lourdes,
a small town in South Western France at the foothills of the Pyrenees
mountains. It is a major Catholic pilgrimage site. Each year millions visit
the Grotto of Massabielle (Grotto of the Apparitions) where in 1858,
the Virgin Mary is said to have appeared to a local woman, Bernadette
Soubirous, who was later canonised. It is the third most important site
of international pilgrimage after Rome and the Holy Land. Over the
years, tales of great and miraculous cures were reported from pilgrims
who bathed in the waters of the grotto. In the grotto, pilgrims can drink
or bathe in water flowing from the sacred spring. I have no idea who
first engaged Betty and Albert in the idea that this may be a way to cure
Albert or indeed, Betty. I have no idea who persuaded her that even after
Albert's death, it would be a good idea to press forward with the plans
and go alone. Perhaps it was Betty herself seeking divine intervention,
solace and guidance in what was now facing her.

Whatever the reason, she set off on the pilgrim alone and grieving
in late September.

With her fellow pilgrims, she dutifully stayed in a local dormitory,
was wheeled up to emotionally moving candlelit ceremonies and was
plunged into the sacred waters over a four-day period.

Did it help? I have no idea. In her absence, Granny Merriman, the ever-present, round, wrinkled, granny of every child's dreams, stayed with us, fed and watered us and guided us back into the school routine with loving kindness.

October 22nd arrived. We were collected from home and driven in a large limousine to attend the memorial concert in The Gaiety. It was a fantastic show. We were seated in the best box overlooking the stage as a parade of artists, most known to us, but some not so well, strutted their stuff and gave their all in a spectacular tribute to one of their own. Artists young and old who had shared the bill with Albert over the years, offered in tribute what they knew best – their talents in entertainment. They too were like Albert. They were ordinary people who had made the stage and their lives all about trying to give a little joy, escapism and laughter to the ordinary lives of their fellow citizens.

Amongst the acts and fellow entertainers that so kindly proffered their services that night were Eamonn Andrews, Pat and Jean, Jim Bartley, Des Smith, Vernon Hayden, Eugene Lambert, Jack Cruise, Frankie Howard, Noel Purcell, Martin Crosby, Cecil Nash, Hal Roach, Gay Byrne, Maureen Potter, Brian O'Connor, Kevin Hilton, Nick Lewis, Chris Curran, Cecil Sheridan, Des Keogh, Austin Gaffney, Liam Nolan, Patricia Cahill and Harry Bailey. The finale act was the combined choirs of The Young Dublin Singers and the whole of the Saint James Church Choir who presented the first Dublin performance of *Let there be Peace*. It was a very emotional and fitting end to the night.

SCENE 6

—❧—

Encore

After the emotive and busy period following Albert's death, things gradually became quieter in the home. Betty carried on caring for the children and became more determined than ever to ensure that she was shaping strong independent women. The motto we lived by became: "You are a le Bas. There is nothing you cannot do." Visitors were not as frequent, with the exception of a few beautiful people who came and chatted to Betty every week. Among them was the lovely Gemma Smith whose husband Con Smith was a long-time non-magical friend of Albert's and fellow colleague in the motor business.

Gemma had sadly lost Con in the tragic Staines air disaster earlier that year. A crash that claimed the lives of 118 people including Con, who was one of a twelve-strong delegation of Ireland's premier businessmen, part of the confederation of Irish industry representatives, who were travelling to Brussels to further Ireland's cause in advance of entering the European Union. Gemma had four beautiful daughters a little younger than us, who came with her on these visits. Together these young widows cried and prayed and built a deep and lasting friendship. Gemma was Italian and a very devoted Catholic. Her presence in those early days helped Betty retain her faith at a time when it would have been so very easy to reject it.

As an aside, in later years through Gemma, we hosted an Italian student on a trip to Ireland for the first time. Her name was Cecillia Fanfani. Her father was an Italian economist and politician, leader of the Italian Christian Democrat Party and Prime Minister of Italy for five separate terms. But I am jumping ahead again!

For Betty, the huge support that she received from family and friends was an invaluable gift. The friends, neighbours, fellow artists and family were the people that populated our youth and childhood, who gave scaffolding to our formative years before and after both Albert and Betty had passed away. This was an eclectic collection of souls who became part of the cloth that we were woven from and their very uniqueness, coupled with Betty's determination, shaped us into the women we are today and for that, I am eternally grateful. Yes, we were pressured to think and act beyond our years, a factor which today would probably be called 'being parentified'. Well done Betty, I say!

The first Christmas after Albert died in 1972, Betty did not prepare the usual Christmas dinner. The ham pot was left to the spiders in the garage. The dining room remained unopened, the curtains shut and the festive table silent and covered with the everyday brown leather covers. Instead, we spent the day with Fred O'Donovan and his lovely wife Sally in their home in Portmarnock, just north of Dublin. It was the first time I ever had a swim on a Christmas Day – in their indoor heated pool!

In the weeks following Albert's death, once again Granny Merriman spent most of the week with us and caught up in our own pity, perhaps it went unnoticed that she was seventy-five years old.

She had shared her daughters' heavy burden during the preceding year and was tired. Akin to Betty, she was a master in keeping her own worries close to her heart and so for a few weeks she said nothing about the nagging pain in her stomach, her loss of appetite and restless sleep, until of course they could not be ignored. She was very unwell. She had to be taken into St Vincent's Hospital where Betty arranged one afternoon to meet with her doctors to discuss her diagnosis and prognosis.

One of the doctors on Granny Merriman's medical team was aware of Albert's death but had never met Betty. I understand that when he saw her in a wheelchair being pushed down the corridor to the appointment, he was unable to sit before her and talk honestly. The next day, that same doctor called in Betty's brother Myles to complete the conversation and deliver the heart-breaking news that Granny had cancer. Just four months after Albert's death, on February 6th, 1973 Granny passed away. As a family, we had lost another guardian angel.

And the grief and rituals of death visited us all over again.

Other changes happened. I was transferred from Sion Hill School back to Rockford Manor, so we could all be together again. As Betty's health declined the following year, another stalwart of a female entered our lives. Her name was Ann Beckett, an Occupational Therapist from the Central Remedial Clinic in Clontarf and she was as energetic, enthusiastic and down to earth a person you could ever meet. Of undetermined age with scattered appearance, a lived-in face devoid of make-up and a wooden leg, she entered Betty's world with a crash.

In no time, she had redesigned the kitchen, drew plans for easier wheelchair access in the bathroom, bedroom and entry doors and just like that, the home was as adapted for wheelchair living as it was possible to be. All the latest technologies were fitted, counter and cooking surfaces lowered and scattered with pull out services and press button gadgets, intercom systems and telephones in every room – all so Betty could maintain what functionality she had and could continue to live as independently as possible in her own home. Within a few years, a tour of our home became part of the syllabus for students of architecture studying in Trinity College and Betty became by an erstwhile tour guide and in progression, a spokeswoman for the Irish Wheelchair Association and the author of a regular column in their association publication. Ann Beckett's presence not only changed our lives physically but on a personal level. Upon leaving school, I too trained as an Occupational Therapist.

The presence of a health professional being so involved in our usually very private life did not herald for us the changes that faced us. Betty's only focus after Albert died was her girls. Yes, she still socialised and on occasion, went out to the theatre or dinner with long-time friend Bryan Ryan or joined us when we went to the pantomime or back to Jurys cabaret but mostly, life was quiet. Dinner dates with friends become less frequent when you are unable to lift cutlery.

Betty's illness progressed. In time, it was clear that we needed to seek help outside the family. Reluctantly, we agreed. A community nurse came to wash and dress her in the mornings, although not every day. I am fairly certain I was the only fourteen-year-old in my class at school that had bathed, dressed and fed her mother, and on occasion, replaced an indwelling catheter, before the nine o'clock school bell rang. Both Louise and Yvonne would have had similar experiences.

It killed Betty to be so dependent, so there was a lot of humour involved in her care – I suppose to mask the reality. By the time she could no longer rely on the use of her arms and had to be fed, we knew we needed to increase the level of care. There was never a second that care anywhere other than in the home she had built with Albert was considered. We got a live-in housekeeper and for a while that worked out. We got a live-in nurse and that worked for a while too. In hindsight, you would have to suspect that an efficient, capable and available nurse who was seeking to live-in with a single patient may have had their own issues and they did. Not for this book, (but perhaps another) are the often hilarious, but mostly frightening, stories of the live-in help that Betty endured when both Louise and I were married, and Yvonne was working in London.

Mostly confined to home, she delighted in visitors from the world of magic. Neville Wiltshire was a favourite visitor and terrific friend. After Albert died, he meticulously catalogued the hundreds of tricks, books and all things magical for Betty and helped organise their sale.

Quintin Reynolds, a younger magician came often, and Betty loved the enthusiasm, the passion and the gossip that he brought with him. Like Neville, he provided an important link to happier days.

Betty held on through several infections and health scares, until her youngest Yvonne was qualified with a degree in economics and a masters from Trinity. She held on until she delighted in, but could not hug her first grandson, Rory McCann and her first granddaughter a year later, Alma O'Leary. She hung tight until she said to herself, 'My job is done'....

On April 29th, 1986 at the age of just fifty-eight, Betty slipped away peacefully with her daughters by her side in St Vincent's Hospital. Away to be with her beloved Albert.

Betty alone had guided her daughters through school and further studies. Luckily, none of us had issues with studies. We were never forced to do better. I suppose because from an early age, the invisible gauntlet was always down – you did not compete against others, only yourself. That and the expectation was that you do your best at all times.

In 1974, Louise began her training as a nurse in St Vincent's Hospital. At the age of twenty-three, this occasional magician's assistant married John McCann. Together, they raised a son and a daughter. Sadly, Louise too would become a widow at a young age, but resilience had been bred into her and she soldiered on. She worked in her profession until her retirement in 2015 and is now revelling in her role as grandmother to two of the most gorgeous children ever born.

I worked for many years as an occupational therapist in Ireland before moving with my husband, Niall O'Leary and our three children to Sydney, Australia in 1995. Here, I also completed a diploma in visual arts and in quiet times, I potter in my art shed. Our three children are grown now. We have produced a nurse, a social worker and a teacher. We could not be prouder of them. The delight of our lives is our beautiful grandchild, Isla Nanlohy. At three, she could already entertain the masses.

Our second-born son Robert, of all the grandchildren, was perhaps sprinkled with the *oofle dust*. He inherited his grandfather's looks and gentle ways. As a social worker, he works a giving and compassionate day job. But at night, this unassuming softly spoken young man plays with a rock band who are currently enjoying quite a level of success on the Sydney music scene. Time will tell where his entertainment dreams will take him.

Yvonne, Albert and Betty's baby, is an accountant. She lives with her husband Len Hremiako in Sydney. She has achieved spectacular success in the area of finance. Like her sisters, she counts her greatest achievement as her two delightful children, Niamh and Finn.

Albert and Betty lie together forever in an unassuming grave under the shade of a dark green yew tree in Deansgrange cemetery. Their final home together marked, not with any elaborate statues or flourishes, just a plain black marble headstone with simple white writing. A passer-by may be forgiven for glancing at the headstone and thinking, 'there lies an ordinary quiet and simple couple.'

I think not.

SCENE 7

Salute

There is a strange thing that happens when you attempt to write about the life of a parent. For starters, your memories are not their memories. Your perception of events and people are viewed through glasses frosted and perhaps distorted by the limitations of childhood and youth. You are challenged to be accurate because all that you know is what has been told to you. You are very conscious that as a child you had no role to question anything. There are few documented accounts of many events in Albert's life, save for a smattering of family holiday pictures and a ton of publicity pictures. There are a couple of precious love letters sent from Albert to Betty whilst he was in the South of France, and a collection of faded and curled Valentine cards with Albert's familiar fountain pen marks showing large question marks and lots of kisses.

Apart from the collection of magazine write ups and pictures, Albert did keep an account of what performances he did and, in some cases, recorded his fees. These were in small annual leather bound and pocket-sized diaries kept meticulously over the years. In one corner of our sitting room, there always stood a mahogany bureau with a flip down leather-lined writing desk with three drawers for important family things.

The top and narrowest drawer held these diaries; each archived in date order and added to at the end of every calendar year. Such a treasure trove of information and history – a catalogue of performances and a tale of a man slowly working towards his life goal to perform with excellence to an increasing amount of people all around the world. Albert's diaries dated back to the 1940s.

For reasons unknown but most probably through grief, not long after Albert died, Betty lit a fire in a metal waste paper bin and burned every one of the diaries with the exception of three – a diary for the year that each of us children were born. Because in each of those diaries was a large excited notation from Albert with the time of each of our births. Her rationale for this was that these books were the story of their lives and were for them alone.

Before embarking on this book, myself and my sisters had several lengthy conversations about whether to proceed. In one respect, we were afraid that we were transgressing some pact made many years before by a couple who had vowed to forever keep their life private. We were tormented that in this book we would be dishonouring Betty's memory and wishes. Eventually, we decided that we would proceed, and we would omit very personal details.

This book would not have happened except for an email I received in early 2018 from Chris Woodward. We had kept in touch over the years and whilst sorting through his magical memorabilia he chanced to find an article about Albert and forwarded it to me. Over the next few weeks, we emailed back and forth daily. One word borrowed another and the idea of gathering all the information we could find on Albert's career, and perhaps turning it into a book, was suggested. Game on!

Were it not for Chris's meticulous research week after week, none of this would have happened. It was the most exciting time. I waited every morning to see if Chris had emailed again, and more often than not, he had. This delightful year of long-distance correspondence eventuated in us meeting on the steps of the London Palladium on September 12th, 2018 – a fitting date as it was the 46th anniversary of Albert's death. It was a magical meeting. There was hugs, tears and laughter. We had lunch and reminisced. His presence brought back so many memories.

I am not sure he will ever fully appreciate what a gift he has given me – the opportunity to open the memory box and once again, delight in the wonder and awe that Albert, Chris and magicians all around the world bring to their audiences every day. I would like to extend my sincere thanks to Chris for all he has done. I know my appreciation is shared by Louise and Yvonne.

Ah my sisters… I am so grateful for their constant input, their corrections and suggestions and the support they have given me while I tried for the first time, to write a book. It is not perfect, I am sure there are dates that are wrong or artists names that have been omitted – if so, I do sincerely apologise.

And finally, this is for my children Alma, Robert and Samuel – that they may know their grandfather and grandmother a little better.

Barbara le Bas
September 2019

SCENE 8

Tributes and Memories

Chris writes...

1972 Patrick Page in his book *Page Boy Speaks* wrote the following, "Let me tell you of another situation relating to the late Albert Le Bas, the Irish Wizard who was a favourite with me and many others.

He was travelling in a train in a carriage holding perhaps six or eight people, one of them was a child. In the course of the journey, to help keep her occupied, Albert showed her one or two magic effects. At one stage, the child suddenly piped up, "If you are a real magician, can you make this train go backwards?"

Ok, so you are magicians – how would you improvise your way out of that one? Because believe it or not Albert made that train travel in the opposite direction, and it took him no more than thirty seconds to do it.

Read that again and try and figure out if you can, how he made that train go backwards on the command of a child.

Have you figured it out? You are probably sitting there with bated breath, saying how the heck did he do it? Ok. Answer coming up now.

After explaining to the child that to do such a magnificent trick, he would have to cast a spell. He said he needed her assistance in this. The child agreed, so Albert blindfolded her with his handkerchief and had her turn round four or five times. During all of this, he had everyone in the carriage change their seats and move their suitcases from one side to the another and when the child opened her eyes and looked out of the carriage window the train was going in the opposite direction.

This delightful 'railway child' story, sadly, of unknown origin was first aired in print in 1972 in the magic magazine *Pabular* by Patrick Page, and then reprised again by John Fisher in the *Paul Daniel's Story* that received a rightful wider general public audience.

In 1987, at the height of the success of TV magician Paul Daniels, John Fisher wrote the first biographical record of Paul's career.

The book was called *Paul Daniels and the Story of Magic* and listed how his career had been influenced by all the famous magicians over the years. John, an extremely knowledgeable author of immense repute, had always admired Albert's work and felt this important book would not be complete without the inclusion of a photograph of Albert and his valuable contribution to International Magic.

Before completing the chapter entitled Magic for that Special Occasion, John reprised that wonderful train story almost verbatim and then added:

'Albert's stage repertoire, like Paul's, was essentially that of the conventional magician's small magic made larger by a personality that lit up the eyes and warmed the hearts of audiences that had seen it all before.'

If Le Bas' whole magical career had been restricted to that one afternoon in a musty train carriage, he would still deserve the special place in Magic's Hall of Fame.

I would like to think that Lewis Carroll would have been happy with this wonderful story too. It has a special and unique charm about it.

Joe O'Donnell remembers...

Back in the old days, Albert frequently toured all the smaller halls with a variety bill which often included Eugene Lambert the ventriloquist. He sadly died some years back and was a close friend of mine. I wrote many puppet shows for his theatre, still gladly in existence, and also the famous 'Wanderly Wagon' in which he played the lead.

Anyway, one night they were playing a run out somewhere in the sticks familiarly known as Ballyslaperdashandmuckery! On this particular night, Betty, Albert's wife and his assistant was taken ill, and Albert was left without an assistant for the big finish to his act. It was the sword box routine done swiftly and with enormous aplomb with about ten long swords, very sharp and shiny. Albert asked Eugene to take Betty's place and Eugene was hugely reluctant. "But Eugene," Bertie pleaded "you know the routine, you've seen it often enough and I'll take my time putting the swords in." They were normally taken from a stand and slammed in – think lightning speed.

Eugene finally agreed, and the big finish came. Albert brought out Eugene and he put him into the box. Eugene, for those who did not know him was a little rotund man, rather stout and heavy set, not in the least like the slim and supple Betty. Eugene squeezed himself into the box and the lid was bolted on and Albert started to insert the swords. Slowly. This was accompanied by muffled groans, and uhs and ahs and the occasional "Oh! Jasus… Go easy Bertie!"

Then came the big finish. Normally the swords were pulled out fast and stuck quivering in the floor of the stage. With difficulty, Bertie slowly pulled out the first sword – it was bent into an almost perfect CIRCLE at which Bertie started to giggle. The other swords were exactly the same. Now Bertie was almost helpless with laughter, as was Eugene. The audience quickly copped on, thought it was part of the act and joined in the laughter. When Eugene finally staggered out pouring with sweat, but otherwise unhurt, there was a tremendous cheer followed by a standing ovation. It was the hit of the show. Albert wanted Eugene to include this as part of the show, but Eugene was having none of it!

Bev Bergeron remembers…

1965 and in Milwaukee, and the last night I got to witness Albert's stage performance. He was right in doing what he did. He was brilliant. It was worth the wait for everyone at the convention to see him. I got to see him perform two more times within a month. Each time I noted what a masterful entertainer he was. In that short period that he visited our states, I got to know the man. I dropped him Christmas notes up until his death.

Several things that impressed me in his act were his use of standard effects but made them his by his original routining. He took a novelty watch that was selling at many of the magic shops back then and worked it into his Rising Card routine. The watch was of the type that has a Polarised disk in it, which as it spun around revealed the face of a card. Albert would have a member of the audience look into the crystal of the watch to reveal the next card to rise up. At first look the watch revealed nothing – so a blank card rose from a glass container. Another look into the watch's crystal and the intended card faded into sight. His magic went on like this until the Miser's Dream. And what a dream it was.

I have seen many magicians attempt to perform the Miser's Dream. Most were a bore as one coin at a time was produced and dropped into a metal container. There were several performers of the Dream that were good. The King, of course, was Al Flosso, but who could match his style that had taken dozens of years to perfect on Coney Island? Then there was Frakson, who could make any magic effect entertaining. No, it was Albert's way of handling the coins and his bucket that set him apart from the rest of the magic world.

He would start out his routine much the same as everyone who had read the book on coin magic by the King of Koins, T Nelson Downs. Yes, one coin was produced from thin air and dropped into the bucket. A loud clang was heard. Trust me, the coin that you saw drop into the bucket was the one that made the noise. The tempo picked up as more and more coins were found 'floating invisibly' about the stage, and then he jumped into the audience and the coins increased in numbers. He was not pulling one coin out of the air, but handfuls. A magical hand would grab a handful of coins from a man's head. Then another handful would drop from an audience member's sleeve. Yes, then he did the nose bit that always gets a laugh – the coins seemingly poured from the spectator's nose and dropped into the bucket. From the right hand and then from his left hand coins seemed to materialize. He never paused to make a steal from underneath his coat or make any moves except to the metal can and then the production. The audience broke into applause – these were hardcore magicians who have seen this trick done to death. In a very short period, he returned to the stage shaking the bucket all the time so that the audience could hear all the coins collected crashing against the sides.

Clang! Clang!

The bucket is set on the table and without a pause each hand reached out to pull down a handful of coins each. As he is dropping them into the bucket, he yells to the audience: "I did pretty well for myself. Not only all these coins, but I picked up a few watches and wallets. As he said these words, he reached into his inside coat pockets and pulled out a handful of watches and wallets, which are tossed into the bucket. Then he takes a well-deserved bow.

Trevor Lewis told me recently that he was a close friend of Albert's and had spent hours with him at a motor repair shop outside Dun Laoghaire, where the ships and ferries berthed from the British Isles. Trevor was head engineer on one of the cross-channel ferries and while waiting for the boat to reload he would spend that time with Albert talking magic. He too was in awe with the man. Trevor learned a lot from the man, especially the Richard Himber Linking Finger Ring routine. Albert worked in Jurys Hotel Dublin almost every night according to Trevor. Trevor's words: "Albert was a superb magician who used magic as a vehicle to entertain. I owe him a lot as he taught me so much. He died far too young."

Chris Woodward was riding around the mid-west of the States when I met Albert. Chris lived near the Irish performer and told me that the man was 'true talent'.

Albert Le Bas was not a full-time magician, but with the many shows that he did in the area, he would more than qualify as one. Sean Brannigan, past president of Ring #85, told me that Albert was one of the founding members of the IBM Ring 85 in Ireland.

Now, I know there are a few of you wondering just what kind of trick metal bucket did Albert use to gather the magic coins? Was it the Abbott version where the large handles allow one coin at a time to drop either into the bucket or into the magician's hands? Was it the one that had a secret hole in the bottom that delivered the coins?

There was no secret bucket or load of hidden coins. What I'm going to tell you was told to the magic world in the covers of the *Gen* magazine in the 1960s and went right past many. Sean Brannigan and Trevor Lewis learned the secret from Albert and used it. I, of course, stole it after I told Albert that I wanted to do so, and he agreed to bless me.

The secret was the rattling of a few coins in the bottom of the bucket. When Albert would pick-up the bucket, he would also fill both hands with as many coins that he could hold in each. Then he would reach out and pull one from the air drop it into the metal bucket with a loud clang. This was repeated over and over until the one hand was empty, then he would switch hands and repeat the movements. With both hands empty he would rattle the can a lot and in the course of shaking the bucket he would jerk the can in such a way that the coins would automatically jump back into the one hand that was holding it. Each time a hand was loaded it would be used to reach out to grab a handful of coins off of someone's body.

He performed this beautiful routine with no gimmicks on the seaside metal bucket and no body gimmicks.

Albert Le Bas was a real magician.

Chris Woodward remembers...

Serendipity is such a beautiful emotive and descriptive word. But for a chance email to Barbara Le Bas and sending her an old image of her dear father Albert, this book might never have been written.

Over the years since the untimely passing of both Albert and Betty, I have kept in touch with both Barbara and Louise, two of their three daughters.

On reflection, I must admit that some of the happiest times of my earlier life and formative years spent in Ireland were amazing and exciting. I feel I owe so much to both Albert and Betty, in particular, and in general, to all the Dublin magicians and the wonderful Irish people that I met and worked with in those seven years or so.

During my all too short a time living and working in Dublin in the late fifties and early sixties, I got to know Albert, Betty, and their growing family very well. Their delightful children, well, I only knew them as just babies or school children. But after Albert passed away so untimely and tragically, it was left solely to Betty to bring up three growing daughters. Whenever I visited, I always but always remember them being immaculately turned out, whether for school or play. A tremendous struggle for Betty in itself especially with the added hardship of living with multiple sclerosis.

I knew Rick Bourke very well as one of the former Variety Club Chief Barkers of the Irish Tent 41 and in a letter to Sir Billy Butlin that I still have, I implored that the Variety Club of Ireland take the Le Bas family under their wing as a very special case, which they did admirably.

Although separated by oceans, the sisters remain very close. Louise a retired nurse, still lives in Dublin. Barbara the second sister now lives in Eastern Australia, as does Yvonne the younger sister with their families. Over the years, we have kept in touch by both snail mail and email. There have been many questions and answers on both sides so happily answered.

To me, he will always be known as Albert, but on sending this Pyke cartoon of 'Bertie', as he was affectionately known by so many, it prompted further delving into my Irish archive.

I suggested to Barbara that perhaps enough material could be gathered together for her to write a book, even a small one, about the 'magic' of the Le Bas family. With very little hesitation, Barbara jumped at the chance asking would I help. Knowing how much Albert influenced my young and later life it was, for me, a way of saying a very big thank-you!

When I first arrived in Dublin, all I knew was the name of Neta Kelly, the then secretary of the Society of Irish Magicians. The SIM was formed in the year in which I was born so I felt an immediate affinity to the club.

Albert was the leading magical entertainer in Dublin, although his day job was with Archers in Dun Laoghaire as a senior executive. His likeable personality showed though at all times. But it was when he donned his tuxedo and fez with a twinkle in his eye, uttered the magic words 'Gilly-Gilly' that he was transformed into another person.

When he walked onto the stage or a cabaret floor, the first impression that anyone in the audience would get was his appearance. He was always, but always, immaculately turned out at all times of the day and night. His magic was also as impeccable as his smart clothes. His Huguenot family origin with a possible 'continental look' and the smart wavy, perhaps even curly hair gave the impression that he could well have been Jewish, but Albert was a staunch Catholic and working for a supportive Protestant company he could and did see all sides of life!

But let's start at the beginning with a huge thanks to our mutual magic friend and Albert's confidante Hubert 'Leprechaun' Lambert. By day, Hubert was a lino-type operator on the Irish Times newspaper but his literary skills and endless knowledge of all things magical allowed him to write copious articles in so many magic magazines. Hubert had been President of the SIM on no less than three occasions:

- 1952-3, during which time the members of the SIM visited The Isle of Man.
- 1953/4 The Convention was in Bettystown and Albert won the Ulster Cup.
- Hubert was President again 1959/60.

Although I had been interested in magic since 1948, during that ten-year period I had, like a sponge, absorbed so much knowledge about people and magic history and was so full of confidence when I arrived on the Dublin scene. I realised quite quickly and in reality, that I knew very little! At best I was just a beginner. In my early days, I was a magician who did tricks that I hope entertained. However, Albert was an entertainer who used the tricks as a vehicle to entertain. There is a vast difference between the two and only experience showed me what that difference was much later!

However, being undaunted, I carried on and I was always chasing but never quite catching up with Albert and his likeable magic touch. He was a pro from head to toe, through and through. If, like a stick of rock, you broke him in half it would read 'honesty, sincerity and entertainment' through the centre. Not only that, he'd had a lifetime's start, Albert had not only appeared on radio, on every stage that Dublin had to offer but on every village hall that each of the twenty-six counties had at its disposal. I'm sure that further research would show that the North and their valuable six counties would also have been on Albert's agenda.

When RTE first broadcast on December 31st, 1961, Albert and his likeable magic appeared on that opening night's inaugural show. He was the right man for job, and it was only right and proper he was honoured with this important accolade. At first, I thought this was his very first TV appearance, but information has come to light from Barbara that tells history differently. It seems that ten years previously Albert had appeared on closed circuit television that was an attraction at the Spring Show held at the RDS grounds in Ballsbridge, Dublin.

The press report of the day makes fascinating reading....

> 'The television tent was a big attraction this morning the only drawback was that people had to queue up in the rain between shows. If ever television does come permanently to Ireland there never need be any fear that there will be not enough talent to keep up entertainment programmes. Viewers today were able to see a very good miniature variety show in which such artists as Roy Croft, compère, and Albert Le Bas, magician, took part. There was also a short fashion parade for the ladies and a film on how television works. The reception for each scene was excellent. The show was relayed from a small studio which had been erected behind the grandstand in the jumping enclosure. A real first for both Albert and TV in Ireland!'

Colour had yet to arrive so naturally television was in black and white, and in a feeble attempt to try catch up (knowing inwardly deep down I never could!) I devised an act of white tie and tails and a silent manipulative black and white theme.

Within three months of that important opening date in the Irish television calendar and following an earlier 'audition' at the nearby Gresham Hotel, the TV producer Burt Budin saw something in my offering that he liked. Contracts were exchanged, and the show was filmed in an old warehouse that was turned into makeshift studios in Henry Street owned by the Bourke family. It was at a time when everyone was learning about this exciting new form of media.

This particular show's theme was honouring the music of Harold Arlen who had written so appropriately *That Old Black Magic*. It was a nerve wracking few hours of rehearsal and transmission, but Albert was the first to congratulate me! I still have his card somewhere.

Prior to the birth of RTE, in the early days television was beamed down from the north with a really snowy picture at times and you had to screw up your eyes to make out who was who. However, once Donnybrook studios were opened officially and as a result of my television baptism, possibly only the second magician to appear on Irish TV, further appearances followed for me. But I was always chasing Albert's tail. I recall being booked for a party in Dun Laoghaire and arriving in good time and announcing that I had come to entertain and with my opening words, "I am the magician". "Oh!" the lady said, "come this way Mr Le Bas!" I smiled but when I told Albert, it really gave him a very big laugh!

This to me, highlighted how well known he was. Today everyone seems to be 'famous' and an 'overnight sensation' – if only for five minutes with seemingly little or no talent. Albert had struggled to earn his 'magical stripes' and he would never have looked upon himself as famous in the strict sense, with all the adulation that would go with fame, but happy to jog along with his quiet fame, taking it all in his stride. He certainly was never conceited, just the opposite in fact, being one of the gang of members of the local society to whom he owed a lot and repaid more than in full for their support.

My only other claim to fame was driving through the O'Connell Street traffic one evening during rush-hour. There was traffic everywhere. The policeman on point duty wearing white gloves and sporting a whistle to emphasise his directions stopped ALL the traffic and walked over to my car. My immediate thought was, 'Well, that's it. I've done something really wrong here…' I nervously wound down my window waiting for an abrupt telling off when the policeman said. "I saw you on the telly last night and thought it was great!" He walked back to his post, blowing his whistle again and waggling his gloved fingers the traffic flowed as normal!

With local television blossoming, the Irish equivalent of *Sunday Night at the Palladium* was created at the Donnybrook studios, where the compère was the ever-genial Albert. The shows were called *Curtain Up* and with Hubert as his magical mentor and advisor, Albert had a flower theme. The series ran for twenty-six weeks and each week he would appear with a brand-new magical item that was flower related and his appearances 'blossomed' as it were! One of his compère favourites was the old Bert Allerton Jumping Flower, where the carnation in his buttonhole would literally jump from one side of his jacket lapel to the other lapel as if by magic. On the next occasion his flower caught fire and, in a flash, it was gone – only to reappear perfectly on the lapel. Goodliffe reported on the show calling Albert's appearances as the 'Gaelic equivalent of Bruce Forsyth's mammoth run'.

Albert's act was a 'work anywhere' show. In the early days of the theatre the audience would be right in front of him, but as the theatres declined and cabaret flourished, this meant a complete rethinking of what to perform as more often than not, you would be completely surrounded on the cabaret floor. It never bothered Albert, he just slotted into his new surroundings like a well-worn glove or shoe. He literally was a true master in his field, borne out of years and years of experience in all sorts of difficult surroundings.

Coins were plucked from thin air, any freely chosen card at random was produced from his pocket, a gas mantle was lit with the aid of a young volunteer who then had milk pouring out of his elbow through a funnel to a waiting jug.

Albert entertained all age groups whether old or young, always with a surprise. I know for a fact that he was engaged for a children's party in nearby Killiney, a wealthy suburb of Dublin. To maintain the suspense, he climbed in through a downstairs window to keep the surprise element for the waiting children. A stroke of genius. As I said, he was a pro of the highest order.

His act was cleverly contained in a specially made suitcase that, at the touch of a button, sprung four sturdy legs, one at each corner and with a deft flick of the hand the case opened, and a table top appeared, and this was his working 'stage'. I still have that suitcase and its own very special carrying case. Inside the bottom of which I have deliberately left untouched as a personal shrine as it contains a business card of Albert's and many deflated balloons that would have been part of his act.

Whether a large card would change its pips as he deftly flicked it back and forth or an even larger offering of a jumbo pack of cards and a liqueur glass, he would say, "Wait til you see the liqueur glass!" as he delved into his table to bring out a ginormous glass that had been specially made for him by Waterford Crystal! Over the years due to the constant work and subsequent damage he had a standing order with Waterford Crystal.

The special pack of Jumbo cards he used was made by John Martin a master mechanic and watchmaker from Lithuania enabling any chosen card to rise. One card would rise, and it was correctly identified, then another but this time back outwards to finally flip over and reveal itself as the second chosen card.

He asked the volunteer to peer into his watch face and asked, "What can you see?"

"Nothing," came the reply and up rose a card that was completely blank.

The last card was reluctant to rise… the Queen of Hearts, in fact it wouldn't rise at all!

Asking the volunteer to say, "Arise your Majesty!" as the freely chosen Queen would magically rise from the pack to tumultuous and well-deserved applause.

Often there would be no musicians available to accompany him but when that facility was on offer he would rehearse and during his show ask, "May I have some Rising Card music, please?" and without a beat or them hitting a note he would say, "Cease the Music!"

Although the object of any magician is to try and baffle you, Albert's aim first and foremost was to entertain and create merriment for you. To transport you away from your everyday working life into a world of suspense, mystery and bafflement.

Everyone who saw his show went away a happier person. By the resultant applause and laughter, he was thankful in the knowledge that he had succeeded.

By day he was a salesman and a successful one at that, and by night he was also a salesman, selling his magical wares, always 101% family entertainment with never anything questionable in his choice or the deliverance of material. That's why he was always in demand and continually working.

In today's world of ripped jeans and tattoos and everything in your face, back in the 60s, they were light years away in terms of dress and behaviour. A collar and tie for work during the day and black tie, or when appropriate sometimes white tie, and patent shoes for night stage wear were *de rigeur*.

Albert was always immaculate whatever the time of day. He expected it of himself just as the public expected it of him.

His approach to performing was subtle and charming. In a word, he had class. That indefinable word where you either have got 'it' or you haven't! Albert had it in seaside bucket loads!

There are few 'real' entertainers today that will be remembered in fifty years' time, as Albert is remembered from fifty years ago. In Ireland, he truly was a shining magical star but selflessly and admirably. He chose family first and in so doing, he denied himself international stardom. How modest, but then that was Albert!

John Fisher chose to acknowledge him in his biography on Paul Daniels because he deserved a rightful place in the pantheon of great names of yesteryear. And rightly so!

On the outskirts of Dublin in Dun Laoghaire, there was a furniture shop called Thompsons. They sold bespoke, and for its day ultra-modern furniture and accessories. As Albert worked in Dun Laoghaire, I'm sure he must have walked past it many times en-route to an appointment or perhaps an eating house for his mid-day lunch. On one of his journeys, he had spotted in their window some rather special lights that were in the shape of a Top Hat. They were made in Sweden and looked very smart.

Now, he could have kept it secret and bought one himself but to highlight Albert's kindness he told me about them thinking they might look nice hanging in my magic den. I still have that red top hat, thanks to Albert's generosity. Just another memory of one of life's givers!

This world as I see it is made up of givers and takers. Albert was emphatically through and through a giver. He repeatedly gave of his knowledge, his time and expertise to those that sought it. He gave of himself to charity when asked and was always at the front of the queue when requests came along. Real charity is wanting nothing in return, not even recognition or publicity.

The most important thing in this world that anyone could wish for is a good name and he certainly had that. No one had a bad word to say about him.

During our Chicago stay we also visited Frank Everhart's 'Ivanhoe' establishment. To access the basement premises, first you need to take the elevator to the floor below the basement level. This special elevator with chains and a mechanism that clunked and groaned as it made its way down to the floors below. The doors opened and there before us was the bar with close-up magic maestro, Frank, in charge. What we hadn't realised was the elevator hadn't really gone down into the bowels of the earth at all. It shook, yes, and gave the impression that it was travelling downwards but in reality, you simply entered through the front door and exited by the back door of the lift that after almost a minute had given the impression of moving downwards. All part of the showmanship of the occasion.

All of us, Albert especially, learned a lot that night. It's not what you do but how you do it! Frank has sadly passed on, but his son Frank Jnr continues the family tradition in Key West Florida presenting bar magic nightly, just as his father had done so successfully before him.

On another evening, the party visited another bar this time owned by Senator Clark Crandall. He was also a master of close-up magic that Chicago was and still is well known for. Crandall wasn't a real senator in the political sense, it was a title he gave himself to add to the character. It was a known fact that when he booked into a hotel unexpectedly to be told the hotel was full, once he mentioned his name, a room surprisingly became available!

What with one thing and another, for us all and for different reasons, it was the most memorable trip.

As magical enthusiasts, we all more or less travel the same journey to find our own individual style and magical personality. Albert was no different. He tried out all the obvious tricks like Card in Balloon, Chinese Sticks and so on. He would naturally have imparted his own thinking and personality into each and every item. None of the items would ever have been wasted in that, although he 'found' his own routine and material that over the years would have been honed to perfection, should he ever be called upon to change his programme, he could. And he often did. He would fall back on those tried and tested routines to fill a needed gap. His many long seasons at Jurys was a perfect example of where he could, at the drop of a magic hat, reprise those old tricks with great success, often with repeat audiences. He knew instinctively what strong performance pieces worked for him and used them to very good effect.

Just as surely as a tightrope walker will miss his footing or a juggler can drop a club, there is an old saying – if it can go wrong, it will.

On one occasion, Albert told me personally that he had prepared and set up the Martin Rising Card pack with the chosen cards ready to rise. He would continue setting up anything and everything else that was necessary for the show, placing them carefully in his magical suitcase. Then came the performance and the cards wouldn't rise. In his haste, he had completely forgotten to wind up the pack! As it was a feature item with no 'out' he simply and promptly took the cards out of the liqueur glass and audibly 'wound up' the cards, getting a laugh in doing so. Bearing in mind he had previously used a 'watch winder' to tell the time so the lay audience would have been none the wiser as to exactly what he was doing!

Night after night (no doubt thanks to Betty's diligence in home care) a clean shirt and polished patent shoes were always the order of the day. Yes, even though patent, the shoes still needed cleaning!

Adrenaline would take over as the overture began. His name was announced off stage and he was away. I always maintain that however long the performance, whether ten or forty minutes, a performer can use up as much energy in that time as a man digging the road for eight hours a day.

You can never switch off until the curtain falls as, after all, you are selling energy! Nothing more, nothing less.

One name within this story appears more than most and that is Goodliffe. He really loved magic and the true worldwide brotherhood that still exists today. He could have been quite insular but whenever there were dates for conventions or special gatherings, he would often include an Irish convention date to promote the wonderful hospitality that one would receive by attending. He spent perhaps more time on his beloved *Abra* than he did on his successful business! If he liked you and your approach to magic, even if you were a humble amateur, he really 'loved' you and did all he could through word of mouth or within his editorial pages to help promote you and your work.

Having researched the *Abracadabra* file since its first issue, Albert's name is mentioned at least once in almost every volume since *Abra* first came onto the magic scene in 1946. Considering there were twenty-six issues in each volume, that was pretty good going. This to me says how much Goodliffe 'loved' and respected Albert and Betty. It is no coincidence that in later life he suffered from MS, as did Betty. However, he could never have known that information in 1946, which highlights that his love for Albert and his work was deep-rooted from the very beginning.

All this research has brought back so many happy memories for me, reminding me of so many wonderful times that I had completely forgotten. Had I not undertaken this project, I would never have known so many facts about my own personal life and travels!

I realise now that whilst I thought I knew both Albert and Betty, I didn't really know them in the fullest sense – I had only scratched the surface. Now, after all this research I feel I have uncovered so much about them both and especially Albert's phenomenal workload. In passing, and when I was really busy my record for one year in Jersey Channel Islands was 410 shows, all within a radius of about forty-five square miles. I'm sure Albert beat me again! See? I never could catch up.

I have lived magic for so many years of my life, I have seen, met, and worked with so many greats and not so greats, but I can think of no other magician whose warmth shone through his work like a beacon of light so powerful that it still shines brightly in all those who remember Albert le Bas. He left behind an enormous legacy in magic that no other magician could possibly fill.

It is apposite here to mention that in 1972, Dai Vernon perhaps sums up what entertainment is all about when he wrote the following in the magic magazine *Gen*:

"To excel at entertaining – the most arduous study, the most genuine talent, the most painstaking effort is not good enough if one's innermost

thoughts are not directed towards aiming to please each onlooker. Every action down to the most trivial must be infused with integrity in its fullest sense – as a man, so he will affect his audience."

Albert's life ended far too soon and there was, and only ever will be, one Gilly-Gilly Man – Albert Le Bas!

SCENE 9

Albert's Favourite Routines

Any Card Called For

There was a famous American magician Arthur Lloyd who created a sensation in Vaudeville when he presented his original routine of 'Any Card Called For'. Simplicity in itself.

A pack of cards was shuffled, divided in two and each half was then placed in each of his trouser pockets. Arthur would then ask for any card from the pack and in an instant, he would produce that particular card from his pocket.

"Any card?" Arthur would call out.

After several playing cards had been produced correctly, a prearranged 'stooge' in the audience called out "Birthday Card!" and Lloyd would then produce a birthday card! This then set the pace for dozens of other types of cards to be requested – membership card, bingo card, business card and so on. The real act would start producing literally any type of card from within his voluminous costume.

As Lloyd's costume was that of a college professor, complete with a flowing gown, it was able to contain enough pockets to house at least 10,000 different cards. Arthur Lloyd's costume complete with all the various cards he could and did produce, now resides in David Copperfield's wonderful museum in Las Vegas.

Albert could see great potential in this idea but would keep it simple and as he would be well versed on the method of simply producing any card called for from within his immaculate suit, he continued

163

to get laugh upon laugh each time another 'card' was requested and produced.

Rather than have thousands of cards, he believed in quality rather than quantity. He would sometimes 'hear' a specific card called for, knowing he could readily produce it. Whereas the production of any card called for was the whole act for Lloyd, Albert chose to simplify the number of cards requested ending on 'hearing' "Placard!" being called for and from the back of his coat would produce a large placard that when opened would simply state, "That's Your Lot!" Tumultuous applause would ensue! I recall seeing Albert do this several times and as with all things in life, simplicity was the key. It always brought lots of laughs as it was humorous in context and content but also very visual.

Balloon Routine

A volunteer was asked to help, and from a selection of colourful balloons that were humorously inflated, one straight from the top to the bottom, another from the bottom to the top, one blown up like a curly spiral, one flying off into the wings.

"Shall I blow it a bit bigger?" asked Albert who then added a little more breath into the balloon. "A bit bigger? Bigger still?" He kept on asking the audience to join in the fun. The volunteer was asked to hold all the balloons one by one, as a way of saying thank you for their assistance in some small recompense. Albert said they would be transformed and shaped into an animal. Albert asked the volunteer to name any animal, but before they could open their lips, "A giraffe!" Albert would say.

Each balloon would be stroked and screeched noisily and moulded, and one by one, deftly and at some speed into a dachshund – a sausage dog, as though this was the 'chosen' animal. Looking dismayed at the dissatisfaction of the volunteer, Albert would then promptly twist and turn all the balloons into a giraffe to laughter and applause, as the rewarded volunteer happily went back to his seat. This was yet another of Albert's signature items. Copied by many, I even attempted to replicate the routine but never quite doing it like Albert did. He managed to extract every ounce of humour, good taste and laughter out of the humble balloon.

Albert Le Bas' Misers Dream by Hubert Lambert

We have just been on the phone with Albert Le Bas, to make sure nothing will be missed in describing for you the routine he uses for 'The Misers Dream'. Having witnessed the sequence very many times over the years, it is still capable of making us sit up in our seats and crane our neck so as not to miss any of the bits of business, and for us, it is infinitely more preferable than 'Dreams' necessitating 'Champagne Pails', all chrome and twiddly knobs and gimmickry.

He uses a child's sand-bucket for the collection, and fifteen pennies, plus one half-crown for the load. The money is in his left trousers pocket with the half-crown 'on top' while the bucket is near at hand, just as is. It is a wide bucket, six inches high and seven inches across the mouth. This is important, as you will see – that short distance from the bottom to the top.

Taking up the bucket and flicking the bottom with a suddenly released half-crown from the thumb and middle finger, Albert announces, "An item with a bucket... and a half-crown!" Another flick, this time with the other hand. "This is the bucket and here is the half-crown," and his left hand goes to his trousers pocket 'in search'. Getting the coins into his hand he, however, 'emotes' failure to find the half-crown, although his hand inside the pocket may be seen to be feverishly 'exploring'. Holding aloft one bucket and looking a trifle sheepish, he says again, "This is the bucket," and out comes the loaded left hand and takes the bucket, while the right hand now dives into that pocket, "and here is the half-crown."

Right hand undertakes embarrassed search for the silver coin, without success. This time is not wasted by the left hand, which gets the coins held under its fingers nicely spread downwards, ready to release the half-crown by the mere relaxing of the middle finger when the time comes.

Taking his right hand from the pocket, Albert tells them, "Well, I'll just use the bucket." He confides, "There's sometimes money floating around in the air, half crowns, pennies and everything. I'll see if there are any here tonight?"

Looking around, he 'sees' one, plucks it from the air and drops it into the bucket. Of course, he has released the half-crown at the moment of drop by the right hand. He is, more or less, surprised at this, so 'pours' the half-crown into his right hand. Using this for several 'visible' productions – from the air, the elbow, knee, etc. The collection is 'on'. About eight is enough, he tells me.

Now a change of pace takes place, for the right hand apparently tosses the coin way up high into the air 'invisibly'! Its flight is followed with the eyes and it lands in the bucket. Once more the coin is seemingly tossed aloft, the flight followed, but there is no sound of anything falling into the bucket. "That was hush money," he explains.

"Let's see if there is any money down amongst you this evening," Albert suggests, and goes down into the audience. At once, by rapid movements from one spot to another, he creates great excitement as he collects, making a great jingling and tinkling with the coins.

All the time the bucket is being joggled up and down, and just as the load of pennies is exhausted from the left hand, a particular 'joggle' causes several of them to bounce up from the bottom to be captured by the free second, third and little fingers, for the bucket is now held twixt only the thumb and first-finger.

When the half-crown is finally dropped, the right-hand fingers receive the 'load' from the left fingers, and Albert is ready to lift a tie here and produce a 'shower' of coins from it into the bucket. Then maybe a single coin or two, followed by several from a handkerchief taken from a spectator's breast-pocket.

Here circumstances play their part, and a bald (good humoured) head may present itself, a lady's handbag, a newspaper, and so on.

Now Albert gives the impression that he collects coins with both hands, but he doesn't. This is brought about by changing the bucket into the right hand as if about to collect with left, but at once a 'better prospect' is seen and the bucket goes back into the original hand, while the right goes to work as before. This is most deceptive and fooled us.

And thus, it goes, the coins being joggled into the left hand while the right is busy collecting, and these being dropped into the right hand as it goes into the bucket with its last coin.

The odd part, as Albert will tell you, is that never is any coin palmed in the classic manner, but just held in the cupped fingers, and 'fed' out.

In the initial part of the journey through the audience, Albert notes a couple of sure-fire laugh 'bits' near the front. Working like a streak among the crowd, he works back towards the stage and uses those 'specials' to get him a good laugh while he makes his way to centre stage facing his audience.

"Let's see how I got on," he says, pouring the coins from the bucket into his hand and pockets them left side. "Not bad," he remarks, ". . . and a couple of watches, too!" Whereon he pulls from his right pocket a 'hank' of watches on chain's, apparently filched during his journey through the auditorium!

Dumping these into the bucket, he takes a bow.

ACKNOWLEDGEMENTS

This book would never have been possible without the enormous help of Neville Wiltshire and also the following friends:

Donald Bevan, Bev Bergeron, Max Blake, David Budd, Dr Michael Colley, L Davenport & Co, John Fisher, Adrian Harris, David Hibberd, Ian Keable, Brad Jacobs, Hubert Lambert, Liam Lambert, Trevor Lewis, Richard Mark, Charles Goodliffe Neale, Joseph O'Donnell, Eustace Malcolm, Ron Pilkington, Tim Reed, Quentin Reynolds, Tony Sadar, Tony Thursby, Louise McCann and Yvonne le Bas.

Albert's name appeared in many magazines but mostly in *Abracadabra*, *Gen* Magazine, *Opus*, *The Magic Circular*, *Pabular*, *The Sphinx*, & *The Linking Ring*.

To them all, we are most grateful and rightfully acknowledge their support and help.

About the Author

Barbara le Bas is the middle child of Albert le Bas. Growing up in Dublin with a magician father and mother who worked as his sidekick in magic performances, she was surrounded by all things magical. To this day, she has never lost her love and fascination for this ancient craft.

Like her father, she sought out new and exciting challenges and in 1995 with her husband and three children she moved to Australia. Barbara lives in Sydney with her husband of 32 years Niall O Leary.

An Occupational Therapist by profession Barbara has dedicated her working life to clients with mental health issues; she currently works as a senior clinician on a mental health crisis team and was awarded a citation by the Premier of NSW (The Bushfire Emergency Citation) for her role in the emergency response effort to combat the 2019-2020 bushfires.

Along the way Barbara has also completed a diploma in visual arts and her paintings have been exhibited in a Sydney gallery.

It has long been on her mind to write this story about a man who nearly 50 years after his death is still regarded as Ireland's foremost magical entertainer. She has finally done it!

Oofle Dust is her first book and tells this magical tale of her father Albert Le Bas.

Chris Woodward

Chris Woodward is a prize winning author with three successful hardbound titles and numerous articles to his credit. Now retired, he was a successful magician entertainer, a Gold Star Member of the Inner Magic Circle - and a member of The Grand Order of Water Rats.

He has also written about and lectured on many cruise ships on the history of The London Palladium theatre as well as speaking in the UK and America on the history of the theatre and famous magicians of the past.

Please Review

Dear Reader,

If you enjoyed this book, would you kindly post a short review on whichever platform you purchased from? Your feedback will make all the difference to getting the word out about this book.

Thank you in advance.

CPSIA information can be obtained
at www.ICGtesting.com
Printed in the USA
LVHW010537021120
670428LV00002B/93

9 781912 328840